COLOR WAR
TIPS, TRICKS AND GREAT IDEAS

THE COLLECTION

This collection of summer camp program ideas came from the submissions of three of our email round tables; "Best Programs", "Best Things We Do At Camp" and "It's a Hit!" These 100 program ideas were chosen because they are unique, creative and most can be done at either a day camp or resident (sleep-away) camp. These activities, programs and events were submitted by directors and program directors from all over the world.

EMAIL ROUND TABLES

Want to be part of future email round tables? Each month a new one is offered. Those on my email list get notified and have a few days to submit their ideas on the given topic. In return they are sent the complete compilation of everyone's ideas. This series of books are edited versions of those round tables. If you would like to participate in future email roundtable go to the home page of SummerCampPro.com and sign-up to receive email notifications.

Curt "Moose" Jackson
SummerCampPro.com

TABLE OF CONTENTS

SETTING UP TEAMS

ODDS AND ENDS

COLOR WAR

Color war is a competition played in summer camps, schools and some social organizations (such as sororities, fraternities, or small businesses). Participants are divided into teams, each of which is assigned a color. The teams compete against each other in challenges and events to earn points. Typical color war challenges include tug-of-war, dodgeball, archery, as well as more contemporary sports such as soccer and basketball. These challenges and events vary based upon the venue for the game. The games' durations can range from a day to several months. The winning team is the one with the most points at the end of the game. Typically, color wars consist of several events that are worth insignificant amounts of points, and then one large final event that is worth enough points to win or lose the entire color war. It is usually at the end of the summer.

Color wars usually begin with a surprise 'color war breakout' to begin, at which point generals and captains are announced. Booklets or flyers are given out dictating teams. Students/campers have meetings and team time periods throughout color war.

Cheers are made up by members of the teams and teams come up with songs to sing and flyers to put up around the location of color war.

At the end of color war, there are presentations such as the teams' banners, songs, skits, multimedia presentations, and team movies. These presentations are worth the most points, and can tip color war in favor of any team. The last day of color war also usually includes some sort of relay races or another large event which the whole team must participate in, also worth a very high number of points.

VIDEOS ONLINE

For visual examples of Color War visit YouTube or Vimeo and search "Camp Color War".
One of the best videos is called Color War 6: The Documentary and can be found by typing the web address below into your web browser's address bar.
https://vimeo.com/50190444

THE COLLECTION

This collection of Color War (a.k.a. Color Olympics, Color Clash, etc.) program ideas came from the submissions of many directors and program directors from all types of camps. Some have been running a version of Color War for years and others are planning their first one. This is an edit version of our Color War roundtable. It contains the best submissions we received.

EMAIL ROUNDTABLES

Want to be part of future round tables? Each month a new email roundtable is offered. Those on the email list get notified and have a few days to submit their ideas on the given topic. In return they are sent the complete compilation of everyone's ideas. The ebooks are edited versions of those round tables. If you would like to participate in future round tables go to the home page of SummerCampPro.com and sign-up to receive email notifications.

Good luck with your Color War, Color Olympics, Color Clash or whatever you decide to call it.

7 TIPS FOR YOUR FIRST COLOR WAR

Starting Color War can be daunting! It is an event that requires a lot of planning and buy-in, which is hard to get for a first-time event. Some of our staff team at YMCA Camp Ockanickon put their heads together to create a list of the top hints for starting Color War. Here's a list of handy tips that will make your Color War a thrilling new tradition and special event for your camp.

Incorporate Established Traditions
At Camp Ockanickon & our sister Camp Matollionequay, we have an age-old boys vs. girls swim across the lake called the Triangle Swim. The winner of the swim keeps the Triangle Trophy at their camp, and now the winner of the swim earns points for their team during Color War. Campers and staff have always loved the Triangle Swim, and suddenly there was a new reason to root for your favorite counselor!

Talk It Up With Your Staff First
If your staff don't love it, your campers won't love it. Talk about it ALL THE TIME. Set reasonable expectations, but talk about it for weeks with your staff before you even bring it up to your campers. If the staff buy in, so will your campers.

Try New Things
Color Wars is our most important special events at camp. However, just doing soccer, basketball, and other normal activities takes away from the excitement because they are done frequently. New activities that you only do during Color Wars can become a new tradition for camp. Last year we created a new game entitled "The Color War." It was a cross between capture the flag and dodge ball with the main objective being that you soak a sponge in your teams color and you throw it down on the opponents colored flag on the opposite side of the field. We were not sure how this was going to work out, but it ended up being the best activity we had all day.

Make It Personal
Color Wars is going to be remembered by campers no matter what. However, what we do is make everyone in a family on the same team, even passing it down to their kids when they are old enough. Once you are on a team, you are on it for life. This is especially important when younger siblings come to camp because they already know what team they are on and are pumped about it.

Split The Day Up
This is a VERY IMPORTANT element that worked out perfectly. Rather than having a 7 year old versus a 15 year old in basketball we split up the age groups by having a younger game and an older game. Most of the older kids wouldn't want to play competitively if little kids were on the court and little kids would have a hard time keeping up with the older ones. For example, our basketball game will first have the younger game then have the older game. Also, we had a practice time in the morning for kids to develop some skills in their activity and create

a bond with their teammates. The afternoon is reserved for competition and the meeting of the teams after lunch is an amazing sight to witness.

Breakout

Breakout for Color Wars is important. Our first year, Color Wars was kept a secret up until the night before the event and it worked out great. However, our second year we spent a week pumping it up and it was even better. We introduced activity coaches, we had a ceremony for new campers who were assigned a team (much like Harry Potter and the sorting hat), and we held an opening ceremony the night before color wars to announce new team captains for the boys and girls on both the black and red teams. The previous boy captains both moved to leadership staff and picked their replacements in the ceremony (the girl captains both stayed as regular staff and kept their captain positions).

Plan Ahead

We started planning for Color Wars three weeks in advance this year and it was still not enough. Color Wars was great, but it can always be better so start planning as soon as possible.

BREAKING COLOR WAR

BASIC AND ELABORATE WAYS
CAMPS ANNOUNCE THEIR COLOR WARS

THE PROPOSAL

I've been part of a "break out" that started with a staff member up on the stage (discreetly wearing one coloured shirt) before a meal - this was normal, as we always had a staff member lead the meal start song. Instead of starting into a song, he called up another staff member, and had her stand on the stage with him. She acted surprised, like she had no idea what was going on. He then proceeded to confess his love to her ("We've been working at camp for 3 summer together and the other season seem too long with out"... etc.) and ultimately ends up proposing!

BUT, before she can say yes, another staff member barges in through the door - obviously distressed, wearing a different colour shirt, yelling for her not to say yes because HE loves her. Lots of theatrics involved, but then the 2nd staff member also proposes. This part can get really cheesey, but also hilarious as the female staff member declares she loves both of them for different reasons, and needs the camp to help her decide via colour wars! She names the two potential fiancées as team captains, naming the teams after the staff (or the colours of their shirts). With this idea, you can close the colours wars with an official proposal, or even a marriage ceremony at closing campfire or at a final banquet dinner. You can go all out for this, decorating and including campers in the wedding.

SCAVENGER HUNT

We have never ran a Color Wars at our programs before but I am defiantly doing one this summer! How I imagine us doing our "break" (based on our location, staff and supplies) would be similar to a scavenger hunt.

The children will receive clues to go to different locations eventually leading them to the cafeteria of our location. At the cafeteria they will arrive into a party like scene with loud music, a PowerPoint presentation being transmitted onto a wall and colors and lights everywhere. This is when we will introduce them to the color wars. They will not find out what team they are on quite yet.

After the presentation and everyone is all excited we will tell them they now have to go hunt for them name card which tells them what color team they are one. Staff will also have to go hunting for their card to figure out what team they will be leading. Once everyone has their colors we will split them up giving them color bandanas to match and paper to make a team sign.

POLICE HELICOPTER

The best color war break we ever did was two years ago when we had a police helicopter land on our field the Friday before we started color wars.

At lunch time the helicopter circled our site a few times before it landed. We kept this a secret from everyone. The kids and staff were so excited and they gathered on the field. The officer handed me a bag of lollipops. I had each child's name attached to the lollipop representing the color team they were on, for example, the cherry lollipops were for campers on the red team.

We had 4 color war teams - red, blue, green and yellow. There were 30 kids on a team and 10 staff. The teams were also given a box. Inside the box were colored bandanas, colored hair spray/paint, a banner, and face paint which they used at the spirit competition which was held on Monday (our first day of competition).

WINTER WONDERLAND

Color War (Olympic) Break for us is one of the most electric events of the summer! Because it is the oldest campers that take part in planning/organizing the break, it is very important to them to keep it secret until the moment it happens. Logistically, this can be a little challenging because most times multiple staff are needed to help coordinate and execute this. One of the lesser complex, but fun Breaks we have had happened 2 summers ago.

The theme for the Break was "Winter Wonderland". The idea was to create an environment that would transform a more secluded, outdoor space near the edge of camp (for secret's sake) in to a winter paradise. Because it was next to impossible to get real snow, we found "Faux Snow". It was a powder that in small amounts gets mixed with water and turns in to something that looks like the fresh powder we were going for. We mixed enough to cover the entire ground. As a back drop, we had an 8'X16' snowflake drop with "Olympics 2011" painted across it. In the field of snow we purchase GIANT (4' in diameter) inflatable balls, filled them with glitter and let them loose.

On the other side of camp, everyone was gathered for a regular all-camp event. The next thing they know, "Winter Wonderland" started playing on the big speakers and the 2 Generals (leaders of each Olympic team) showed up out of nowhere, decked out head to toe in their team's color, riding on the back of a golf cart. At this point everyone realizes what is happening, starts screaming and chases the Generals to the snow-filled field. Upon arrival, music is rocking, the bubble machine was blowing and everyone started dancing and playing in the snow. To top it off, an ice-cream-truck-decorated camp van pulled up and handed out snow cones out of the back (a logistical feat in and of itself!). After the initial shock wore down, teams were announced, the Generals gave their speeches and the 2011 Olympics commenced.

FIREBALL

I have never seen this personally, but have heard about having a fireball that starts the camp fire. I heard from a friend that the counselors at their camp took a paper towel roll and wrapped it with lint, toilet paper (and anything else flammable) and some wax to cover it in. Before the campfire session starts, some one builds up the wood in the fire pit, and runs a wire from the camp fire up to a tree in the background. When ready for the campfire session to start, and a staff member has made the grand opening, the fireball is lit, and glides down the wire to the fire pit where the big fire is lit. [Again, I cannot personally vouch for this method, so my suggestion would be to try it out before the big night!]

BREAKING NEWS

We sent home an email to the staff and parents telling them we are working on a new camp video and will be having a screening when it is complete. On the day of the screening we gather the entire camp body into our rec hall where there is a giant TV screen. We play the video – for about 5 minutes the entire camp is viewing a montage of pictures from the previous years.

At a certain point – the video stops – and on comes a TV news announcer (this was a real news anchor) – saying they interrupt this broadcast to announce there is a villain on the loose at Tall Pines and Uncle Andrew has called in the heroes to see who can destroy the villain first. On the screen are the characters from each side – which we previously filmed – of them running through camp; Then suddenly and timed perfectly they burst through the doors of the rec hall and run through the crowd with confetti guns.

http://bit.ly/1Emd199
(The news breaks in at around the 3 minute mark.)

Once the crowd is calmed down the generals then announce which bunks will be assigned to what color – then green and white bandannas are disbursed to each bunk counselor to give out. Also the entire weeks activities are given out in a day by day schedule.

HOT RODS

To Break Color Wars, it would be awesome to setup a street race! Have hot rods or sports cars that make a lot of noise that have the same color as the teams! I can picture all the campers cheering and getting excited as the cars rev engines for a couple minutes! We count down from 5 seconds to start the race! Then finally they take off to break Color Wars! Speed boats on the lake or ocean would also work! So would loud dirt bikes in the mountains!

IT'S MAGIC

My favorite recent break involved creating a "set" for an outside performer (a magician in this case) using large appliance boxes. The captains were hidden in the boxes before the show. At the end of the performance, a staff member came on stage, thanked the performer, and then segued into the surprise introduction of the theme and captains. Our color games (and we call them "games" not "wars" on purpose) always have a theme and back story. Some years this aspect is more elaborate than others.

FLASH MOB

Have two marching bands show up out of the blue then 'face off' and end with them holding up coloured banners.

Have an open house day and then all of the guests turn into a flash mob, who take off their shirts and are wearing tank tops that are the colours. (I'm thinking like the Black Eyed Peas flash mob on Oprah. Also are flash mobs passé now? I don't have any of my counselors around to tell me I'm not cool anymore – so it's sometimes hard to judge! Haha) Or it doesn't have to be an open house day, alumni, etc. could just show up in a colorful flash mob.

FALSE BREAKS

There are things called fake or false breaks which can be more fun than the real break. A fake break is where you pretend to break color war. At one of the camps I was at for color war, color war could only start if the director crossed the two hatchets of the two colors of the teams. So he would sometimes cross two hatchets of the same color or someone else would cross them. None of these counted. The fake break can be as elaborate as the real break to get everyone excited.

One of the fake breaks was started in the middle of the night. During the alarm everyone was gathered on the beach. While on the beach a pirate ship docked on the dock and pirates surrounded the campers screaming and asking about the hatchet. Their master the, evil pirate Black Beard, threatened to torture us all until we gave up the hatchet. When no one gave him the hatchet he separated everyone into groups by age then had them perform some team building exercises as "torture" then said he was tired and would come back in the morning to continue looking for the hatchets.

Basically fake breaks create hype for the actual event and can be themed on whatever is popular of different for that summer. However I have found that the real break is often a not related. For example pirates could come for a week, but the real break could be about Batman or Spiderman.

CAMP IS CLOSING

(If you're opposed to tricking your campers, this might not be a good one for you) Start a 'rumor' that the camp is being shut down. Make sure that everyone knows the 'secret info' and that the director is going to be on the local news doing an interview or press conference. Then have the senior staff let the campers and staff watch the news, because they know they've heard the rumors and they should probably hear it for themselves. The director could start out being solemn and pretending it's going to be bad news then start yelling with excitement to break the games. It could probably be taped in advance so it wouldn't be on the actual news.

COLOR WAR FAKES and BREAKS

This is one of the biggest moments to me, this is what I spend 10 months of the year putting together trying to make it more amazing each summer.

Let's talk about fakes. This is when I do something crazy where the camps think color war is about the break and then I have a banner that comes out saying fake out. You should see the kids; they are sitting on the edge of their seats each day waiting for it to start. We do some fakes that cost nothing, to cost a little.

Each year I have a tradition where I play music and call all campers and staff to the gym. I have a boys vs. girls comp - treasure hunt. Each bunk is given a clue to find part of the puzzle; they then bring it back to the gym and start to put everything together, which will show a picture - A picture which is a clue to the names of color war. We give out clues throughout all the fake outs so the campers can try and guess what the color war names are going to be. I also have a CD with sound effects.

The best is the helicopter, you wouldn't believe how you play the sound of a helicopter over the PA system, then say everyone go to the girls tennis courts, and 450 (campers and staff) drop everything and run, and then there is nothing there. Try it. We also have put food coloring in the milk blue and yellow at breakfast, left clues on everyone's bed when they are at a meal, so when they come back they go nuts. We have made funny movies on camp, woke the kids up at 1am and showed them. One year we took the banner and filmed the banner at places the kids and staff know, like Walmart, Chinese, bowling alley, movies, our day camp etc. Asking them if they know where the banner is, it's pretty funny and costs nothing.

I have taken 5 male counselors, and put a funny dance in the pool to funny girly music, had counselors paint their body blue and yellow and run around camp. I even have two morphs suits that we use each summer, with clues. Last summer we even got a child morph suit, so it was like a color morph family.

I have had a scuba diver go into our lake while kids are still sleeping, called all kids to the lake and then randomly out walks this scuba diver with a clue. This year I also took my Waiters/Waitresses (10th graders) I did a glow in the dark dance with them, right before the break, so our kids thought for sure it was the break, then had a sign saying fake out. I have had a fire truck come on camp, police car, even a bus pull up and off walked my director dressed up as the old man from six flags and started dancing to the music.

Last summer I had a dance group come on camp, after we told the kids someone stole the banner and we needed it back or we wouldn't do color war. The dance group came running in saying they stole the banner and if we wanted it back we would have to do a dance off. I have had a hummer limo drive on camp kids thinking someone famous was in it and then the morph suits come running out. I have so many, please email me any questions or pictures/videos.

BREAK OUTS

This is my baby, past 6 years I am the one researching and booking the event. This does cost some money, however you do not need to spend any ideas from my fakeouts can also be used as a break out. Here are some past color war break:

Jousting Competition
At 9pm, kids were led from our gym to our sitting area. Two horses were waiting and then announced the black knight vs. the blue/yellow knight. We then walked over to our soccer fields, where they started the competition, jousting, sword fighting, very exciting.

Fire Cirque du Soleil
Took all our campers off camp for 3 hours to our day camp, in the mean time the company set up in our gym. Campers came back and we paged them to the gym. different fire effects, hula hoop, head gear, even lit part of the (cement floor) gym floor on fire, had a large hoop attached to roof and performed while the hoop was on fire. AMAZING BREAK!

Helicopter/Skydivers
Helicopter flew over our soccer fields, and dropped paper, paper put together said "Is this it?". Then a guy rapelled out of the helicopter with smoke. Then 3 sky divers jumped out, helicopter then flew to other side of camp and picked up our morph suit people, after skydivers landed flew back and out run the morph suit people with the color war booklet.

Lazer show
Had the campers on the upper hill on camp while lazer show set up, campers couldn't see. Campers went back to their bunks then paged at 9.30pm to the gym. As they walked in gave them glow sticks. There was a little fog in the gym and campers sat on ground. Then the lazer show began showing pictures related to the team names, kids got very excited.

Megasarus
This was crazy. We had a car parked at arts and crafts one day. Made announcements who ever owned the car to move it or we would have it towed. Next day paged campers to sitting area, then the Megasarus drove onto camp, opened up and the dino came out of the top. It then, with its arms, picked up the car and the dino (breathing fire in the air) bit into the car tearing it into pieces.

Monster Truck
Had two cars at top of hill. We would sneak bunk by bunk up to the cars and have the boys paint one car blue and the girls paint one car gold/yellow. Then next day we moved the two cars to another location. We later escorted our campers to this location. When they got there all they could see was the two cars that they had painted. Next minute the monster truck (they couldn't see) turn on its engine, and out roaring came the monster truck that then smashed up the two cars. Crazy to see and kids loved this

Newspapers
We had all the kids taken off camp and while they were off camp we put 100's of newspapers

that were designed for us just for color war, spread out all over girl's side. When they returned the kids went running picking up the newspaper and reading what team they were on, color war names etc.

SKITS

The camp I have been working at for the past two years does do a sort of Color War. The teams are created by the admin staff so that they were fair. Lists with kid's names and assigned color were given to staff.

The first year: Skit
The Color War broke out in a sort of skit done by the program staff. It was Pirate Week so the "Pirates" stole some of the camper's lunches (these were just bags that looked like real lunches), and tried to kayak away across the lake (everyone was having a picnic lunch at the lake). The cook, of course, could not let the Pirates steal all of the lunches from the camp so she jumped in a kayak and began to chase the pirates. There was a sword/wooden spoon fight on the lake and the pirates were tipped out of their canoe. The lunches were saved, and a box of bandannas with the color war list was discovered in the canoe.

The second year: Skit and All-camp activity
The color war happened during the Hunger Games week. Basically, the Program Staff did another skit but this time they were dressed as Peacekeepers. During dessert after dinner they stormed in and announced they were taking over the camp and that they had stolen all of the bandannas that had been promised to each camper. This skit then turned into an All-camp activity.

Peacekeepers went to their assigned stations all over camp. Each Peacekeeper was armed with a squirt-gun and their job was to protect their bandanna stash. The Peacekeepers could not hold or touch the bandannas and they had to be placed in an area that was easily accessible to the campers. So Peacekeepers could hang them on a clothesline or place them on a picnic table or something and then just guard the area.

Each camper had to capture a bandanna of the color that was assigned to them (counselors were telling each camper which color they had to get while Peacekeepers were setting up their station) Campers could only capture ONE bandanna that was their assigned color. They could help other campers capture their colors by distracting the Peacekeepers, but they could not touch another person's bandanna. Some of them got pretty creative with camouflage or other distractions.

The Peacekeepers could squirt campers with the squirt-guns. If a camper was squirted, the camper had to leave that station and try to get their bandanna color from another station before returning to try again. If the camper had captured a bandanna but had been squirted during or even after the capture, the camper had to give their bandanna back to the Peacekeeper (even if they did not steal it from that particular Peacekeeper).

Once everyone got their bandanna, they all met in the Dining Hall, and then Seneca Crane came for a surprise visit. He then told them that their Color teams would help them compete in the

Hunger Games later that week. It was just more group competitions that were Hunger Games themed.

I don't remember if the program staff came up with this All-Camp or if they took it off the internet somewhere, but the kids seemed to really like it.

THE CAMPERS ARE THE STARS

We've had some great Color War "Breakouts" over the years at our camp, but I think this one takes the cake.

Lots of camps break out Color War with a visit by a big movie star or celebrity (or, more often, a celebrity look-alike). Well, we decided to be creative and flip it around - we made the campers the stars! Here's how:

Earlier in the week, we filmed campers dancing at camp. Then we spliced the footage into a normal movie (we used 'Madagascar'). On the big day, we had the whole camp watch the movie. For the first few minutes nothing seemed out of the ordinary...but then, right in the big party and dance scene, all of a sudden the campers saw THEMSELVES, right there on the big screen, STARRING IN THE MOVIE!!!

Naturally, the whole pace went nuts! The campers were amazed, and the cheering and yelling was so loud and incredible, I don't now how we could have announced anything audibly at that point - luckily we had edited it so the screen switched to big flashing text that said "Color War Breakout!!!"

It became an instant legendary camp classic, and I don't now how we'll ever top that "breakout" - but that's part of the fun of Color War!

VARIOUS IDEAS

- A Bear Scare – Camp was gathered to announce a bear sighting...many tears ensued!
- The couple that owned the camp had a big fight in front of the whole camp
- Colored ribbons were placed under the plates at breakfast
- Campers awoke to find a stripe on their forehead
- A helicopter buzzes the camp with the owner in it
- For Cowboys and Indians, we ran to an upper field rarely used to find professional stunt riders.
- Another year was a high wire act.
- Sky Divers - If you don't want to have the real generals sky dive, have the professional sky divers land just off the area where all the campers are. Then have the generals "planted" in sky diver outfits (goggles and all...hair messed up from the wind) and run into the area where the campers are. They will never know the difference
- Monster Trucks
- Old Fashioned Cars and Trolleys
- Tricked out cars and limos, etc.

- Camels (this was cool)
- Drop fortune cookies from an helicopter with a message inside about color war
- Have a staff basketball game that most of the camp or all of the camp is watching. Midway through the game, some goes down in pain. A call is made to an ambulance. The ambulance arrives and out of the back comes the generals.

EASTER EGGS

If you have a gator (or vehicle-type) lawnmower or go-cart to ride, you can ride through camp and throw out those plastic Easter eggs that are filled with a piece of candy that says, "Color Wars is on!" or "Sweet! It's Color Wars Time!" Or you can make it a message that a camp or bunk has to piece together...they would have to open each plastic egg and work together to put together the message (or even a coded message) that says that Color Wars is on!

S.W.A.T. RAID

We have a fantastic connection with our SWAT/TACT team in our community. On the first day of camp after check in arrange a group outside activity. In swarms the swat team and possibly the police helicopter flying above the crowd of kids. The swat team will be armed with very obvious.... water guns full of coloured water! They will shoot the groups with the colours that they will be. With either the team or helicopter above announcing "let the colour wars begin!!!" After the pandemonium of what's going on cools, Captains and generals will be announced and colour wars will kick off!

BLACK LIGHT DANCE

This year we are going to have a black light dance and of course pass out color glow necklaces but to make it more exciting I ordered invisible markers that can only be seen under black light. Once we have the teams staff will put an x on each campers hand, which they will not be able to see until the dance.

We will make the announcement to look at the X on their hand and those will be the teams.

SPORTS CENTER

One of the most outlandish ways I have seen to break the color war was on sports center. The camp director is a good friend of one of the announcers of the show. So during the end of the show he made an announcement about an upcoming sporting event that he was sure to excite a very special group of kids. Then he played a video of the camp director crossing the two hatchets on live TV. So at camp the kids were are all watching sports center having been told that it was some baseball game they were supposed to have been at but was canceled because the buses were broken. Everyone was one in complete amazement.

ALIEN CRASH LANDING

Have some of the staff build UFO wreckage deep in the woods at camp that campers are not often in. Then create a trail along the way very much like a haunter forest idea. Random parts scattered in the woods. Spread the inside glow sticks to make appear as alien blood. Have some of the counselors jump out dressed as aliens along the way. Then sound the alarm and gather all the campers and have them march to the wreckage.

Once every has arrived have the alien emerges with one of the hatchets. He could warn the campers that a dark force was coming and there camp would be the battle ground for the fate of the cosmos. On the way back to the cabins have the campers stop by the field in time for a skydiver to land dressed as the forwarded alien force. The two aliens can meet up and cross the hatchets and start the color war.

FIRE AND ICE

Color Wars at my Camp is the most anticipated Week of Summer. When it comes to special events we don't hold back! We are 110% when it comes to Color War every summer. We live 10 months out of the year counting down to the 2 months of camp and the 4 days of COLOR WAR. We have come up with amazing themes and amazing breaks but the one that stands out and if it can be replicated to the degree we did it then OMG this is the Break to do.

The Theme was Fire & Ice
I started off by contacting our local fire department and police station and held a secretive meeting explaining Color War and what it means to our camp and asked them if would help us out.

One team was going to be FIRE and the other ICE. There are so many minor details of how this BREAK played out and whoever decides to try it, I am here to go through everything.

My next step after meeting with the fireman/Police was to let them know my needs from them. Let me set the stage - our camp is on 15 acres, 700 kids. We have a huge rock wall on our field which is going to play an active role in the break.

It was 8:35 am...all the buses had arrived and all the children were heading to their arrival areas to have attendance taken. (Every little detail was thought about and considered and planned down to the last detail.)

Signal was given. We were ready. Fire alarms started going off. They were sounding from the top of our camp to the very south end. Kids knew the routine of meeting down on the field to have a head count done and to await further instructions. Kids weren't sure if this was a fire drill or real fire until…they began to see smoke arise from one of our buildings (smoke machines were provided by fire department. They use the smoke machines for drills. They look and smell real.

One building went up in smoke, fire alarms going off, controlled chaos down at the fields where all the kids are assembled waiting to see what is going on. Next thing everyone hears is a countless number of explosions where they see one building after another go up in smoke.

Within 3 minutes 4 fire trucks arrive. Inside the truck are the generals of the FIRE team as well as the fireman and they enter the north side of the camp. (This is all staged.) They get out of the trucks, pull out their hoses and start to hose down the buildings... in full gear.

As the kids are watching from 200 feet away the rock wall which is about 100 ft away from the kids begins to rumble and starts to make creaking noises. (We have a sound system set up at Bungee which is right next to the rock wall, and the rock wall is controlled by a remote control when it moves up and down.) Kids are freaking and don't know which way to look - at the fireman trying to put the fire out or the rock wall which looks and sound like it is about to explode.

The rock wall all of a sudden starts to go down slowly with smoke barreling out, looks as though its coming crashing down.

At that very moment 6 cop cars (with ICE Generals in cars as well as police officers) come barreling in with lights and sirens from the opposite end of camp.

Timed perfectly The fire trucks and police cars meet up at the rock wall just as it appeared to crash to the ground and BLUE and ORANGE colored smoke bombs were released from top of the rock wall along with blue and orange balloons from everywhere on campus. BLUE & ORANGE ARE OUR CAMP COLORS AND THE CLUE THAT THIS MEANS IT'S COLOR WAR and indicates the start of Color War.

I have never heard screams from kids like it - the relief that the fires weren't real to seeing their favorite Group leaders as generals and lieutenants jumping off fire trucks and out of police Cars running towards them.

It was perfect, looked as though it was a scene out of Hollywood and worth all the work and stress I may have endured. The kids have been saying that it was THE BEST, SCARIEST and UNSUSPECTING COLOR WAR BREAK they have ever had

HITS AND MISSES

Color War at our camp is a big deal. Many campers actually schedule the weeks they want to be in camp around when they think color war will be. Each year it comes out at a different time.

- One year we told the kids the night before that a player from a sports team was coming. This turned out to be a mistake as parents sent their kids with sports memorabilia to be signed and it got ruined in a few cases. Also the fact that I showed up in drag from a limo led to boos from the campers. I hope everyone can learn from my mistakes.
- We had a sheriff come and teach us about what to do if a bear was spotted and while he was speaking, someone in a bear costume came up to the pavilion holding a COLOR WAR BANNER
- We told people a special musical guest was coming. Somehow, it spread that Justin Bieber was coming. A stretch hummer limo pulled up, the driver rolled out a red carpet and the Color War Generals exited (much to the dismay of the teenage girls but they took it well!)
- We hired a pilot in a small plane to drop BLUE papers and RED papers (that had COLOR WAR printed on them) over our camp. You may think clean up was hard but we made that our 1st event. The team that picked up the most papers won the event.
- One year we played Lets Make a Deal and one of the boxes held helium balloons and a banner that announced color war.

DREAM BREAK OUTS! I would love to hire a helicopter to hover over camp and have someone rappel out or a sky-diver jump with smoke trails into camp!

INDEPENDENCE DAY

We have done our Color Wars for the last 6 years with much success. As they've evolved over the years, one thing is consistent, it's all about full inclusion over every village and every age group.

Last year was probably the best year we had for one of our "breaks", we do 2 color wars every season. Our color wars was on the 4th of July, so our "break" was on the evening of July 3rd. Our teams were Red, White and Blue. Red symbolized the Bald Eagle, Blue, Uncle Sam and White, the Statue of Liberty. Well, incorporating an Independence Day movie theme with the Aliens coming down to take away America's Independence and attack The Bald Eagle, Uncle Sam and Statue of Liberty.

We made an announcement for an all Camp meeting on the Beach. Program Staff dressed as the patriotic and alien characters. The patriotic staff made it seem as if it was an introduction to the 4th with poems, music, etc and to hype everyone up. An interruption occurred; the Aliens chased away the patriots and were taking over July 4th, a new independence day, the Alien independence. A mock battle ensued between the Aliens and our patriots and the Aliens vowed to return for their revenge as they were chased off the beach.

On our floating dock we constructed a chicken wire panel that had burlap, soaked in diesel and spelled out "Color War"... the Patriots lit the burlap which igniting and lit up the night, floating off of the water the announcement of the 2013 Color War.

PART
2

COMPETITIONS

GAMES, RELAYS, HUNTS AND OTHER
COMPETITIVE WAYS TO EARN POINTS

CARDBOARD REGATTA

One week we found ourselves with a large excess of cardboard. We divided it between the 5 groups and gave them 1 roll of masking tape and an hour. They were instructed to build a boat/craft that would carry at least 2 people. At the end of the hour, we took the crafts to the pool and had a race to the other side of the pool and back. Most of the boats sank halfway down to the other side, but 1 made it to the other end before sinking.

CAPTURE THE FLAG VARIATION

We have also done a sort of Capture the Flag. We had 2 people serve as "flags" for each team- 1 Camp Director and 1 Unit Leader- and each team hid their people in separate locations on the property. Then the teams raced to find the opposing team's people. We did this challenge in the evening and provided flashlights to the teams. The search lasted a couple of hours.

MONSTER RELAY

This is a camp wide relay in which teams sign up their campers to complete one leg of the multi-legged race. We try to have a wide range of activities for this so all campers can contribute -- running, egg on spoon walk, 3 legged walk, speed beading, trivia, canoeing, kayaking, archery, rolling down a hill, spelling, giving 5 beaver facts, 3 cartwheels, etc. The last leg of the race is almost always fire building, or canoeing to a beach where they grab a flag and place on top of a sand hill. We often make the Monster Relay a triple point event!

Do a staff challenge as a double point event! Could be anything -- a volleyball game during rest hour, a spelling contest during dinner, or event a monster relay!

GREEK WEEK

My connection to Color Wars is from college. I am in a sorority and during Greek Week would have color wars. Each event that we participated in was worth so many points and at the end of the week, the group with the most points was awarded the winner of Greek Week with t-shirts and cups and other fun stuff. Some of the events that we participated in were:

- Tug-of-War
- Dodgeball
- Basketball
- Scavenger Hunt
- Flag Football
- Hot Dog Eating Contest

WET SHIRT RELAY

- Put a t-shirt at the other end of your shallow dock down at the lake.
- Divide the group into four teams, and have each team line up on the beach.

- Once the race begins, the first member runs to the dock, puts on the wet t-shirt, and runs back to his/her team. When he/she reaches the team, he/she removes the shirt and gives it to the next person.
- The next person puts on the shirt and runs to the dock, takes off the shirt, puts it back on the dock and runs back to their team.
- The first team to have all players finish the task wins!

BEACH TOWEL VOLLEYBALL
- Form 2 teams.
- Have each team stand on either side of the volleyball net.
- Have each team divide into pairs.
- Each pair should have one towel and each person should grab 2 corners of the towel so that it is spread out between the pair.
- A water balloon is placed on the towel of one of the pairs.
- The pair must then work together to lift their towel so that the balloon is propelled into the air, across the net to the other team.
- One of the pairs on the other team must then try to catch the balloon with their towel and return it the same way.

As in regular volleyball, a team scores a point when the balloon hits the ground on the other side of the net. Like Volleyball the object is to score the most points and get the other team wet at the same time.

COUNSELOR HUNT
Our finale each summer is a counselor hunt. We allow our senior staff and specialist to hide somewhere on our camp site. We give them each an envelope that they are not allowed to open. Each envelope had an amount from 50 pts - 500 pts. The campers are given 20 minutes to find as many staff as they can. At the end of the hunt we all gather and open the envelopes to see which team has the most points.

SPLAT!
This is a team building game and very messy.
Materials:
- sponges (variety of sizes)
- 2 buckets (for the paint)
- 2 flags
- safety goggles
- lots of Tempura paint (Different colors for teams represented per game- MAKE SURE YOU PURCHASE WASHABLE TEMPURA PAINT) You can water down the paint to make it last longer.

The object is very simple it's a game of capture the flag (played in 15min increments) but there is a catch - when you are hit by another teams paint covered sponge you are now apart of that team. Once the 15min is up or if one team has captured the other teams flag (award that team with 50 points) count and see what team has the most players on it than award that team 100 points (Points can be altered to your liking). This is a very fun messy game that the kid's absolutely love.

SOCK WRESTLING

You need two socks. Use mattresses to act as pads, multiple arenas should be created. Any camper that wants to go will have a chance. Each match is limited to 3 minutes. Each camper will place a sock on one foot. No biting, scratching, hair pulling, or anything to do with the face, the goal is to get the opponents'' sock off and keep yours on. This is also really fun for campers when staff compete and campers watch.

COUNSELOR BOWLING

Use a scooter and items to act as bowling pins (water bottles, empty gallon ice cream containers stacked up, etc.), Staff members act as the bowling ball by sitting on the scooter. Campers push their counselor down the designated lane at the 'bowling pins'. Give points based on the number of pins knocked down. Be sure to set up a crash pad behind the bowling pins - we use mattresses leaned against a wall. Campers and staff love this activity!

JELLO TOSS

Materials Needed:
- plastic bowl attached to the top of a helmet
- pre-made jello (a lot)
- Dixie cups

Goal:
To get as much jello tossed into the bowl, as possible.

Directions:
- In traditional relay fashion, have each team line up at a "starting line."
- A counselor (or a CIT) from each team is to wear the helmet (with the bowl attached to the top, so that the flat bottom of the bowl is attached to the top of the helmet), and kneel a few yards away from their team.
- Before play begins, each staff member uses the Dixie cup to scoop out a handful of Jello and give it to each camper.
- When play begins, each camper takes a turn throwing the Jello, with the goal of getting as much in the bowl as possible.

The winning team earns a point!

MARSHMALLOW TOSS

Materials Needed:
- large marshmallows
- pudding

Goal:

For the team to "catch" as many marshmallows in their mouth as possible.

Directions:

Campers line up with their team, at the start point.

A few yards away, a camper is kneeling, waiting to try to catch the marshmallow in their mouth.

As the campers approach the start line, they are given a marshmallow to dunk in the pudding, then throw at their team mate.

Once a camper has thrown, it is their turn to go out and try to catch the 'mallow.

The team with the most catches earns a point!

COCOA PUFF TOSS

Materials Needed:
- (Sensitive Skin) Shaving Cream
- Cocoa Puffs (or any round-ish cereal; stale cereal from the Dining Hall works, too!)

Goal:

To cover your counselor's face in the most pieces of cereal.

Directions:
- Campers line up with their teams, at a start point.
- A counselor from the team smears shaving cream all over their face, and kneels a few yards away.
- Each camper is given a handful of cereal to throw at their counselor.

The counselor with the most pieces of cereal stuck to their face wins a point for their team!

EGG DROP

Materials:
- Eggs (uncooked)
- Materials to "construct" with (such as masking tape, straws, popsicle sticks, ribbon, yarn, coffee filters, small boxes and bottles, toilet paper rolls, etc.)

Goal:

Get your egg safely to the bottom of the Climbing Wall (or other tall structure/staircase).

Directions:
- Give each team an egg, and equal amounts of materials to which they will construct their "safety device" with.

- Let each team know that the goal is to keep the egg safe, without attaching anything to the egg (so no taping bubble wrap to it!).
- Therefore, they need to build a vehicle that will deliver the egg safely to the ground from the top of a specified height. Give the campers a time limit to build such vehicle; between 20-40 minutes, progress depending on the groups.
- Once the construction time is up, have the campers bring their egg and vehicle to the determined spot.
- Ask a "neutral" staff to drop the creations from the specified height. (Dropping the eggs from the top of the Climbing Wall was the highlight of the day for many campers!)

Points are awarded based on qualities such as the extent to which the shell was cracked (or not) and creativity in the vehicle design.

CABIN GRAB

Cabins are told to run back to their cabin and grab as many items as they can bring out in one trip. Give them a FAST time limit like 2 minutes (depending on how far they have to run!) Be creative and pick things you think no other groups will have!

They return and group with their team/cabin. The game leader then yells out an object from their "list" (can be a real, pre-written list, or a cheat list where the leader spots items groups have brought out and says those), and teams must show they have that item, or a similar item.

It's sort of like a reverse scavenger hunt. If teams prove they have that item, a point is given. Game can be short or long, depending on time needed!

OVER LAND/OVER SEA and SING DOWN

We always end our games with two events: a huge camp-wide relay race called "Over Land/ Over Sea" (OL/OS) and a "Sing Down".

For OL/OS, teams of campers are placed all over camp with tasks to complete. A junior counselor from each team runs from group-to-group in a specific order followed by an entourage of captains, "officials", the camp photographer, etc. As each event is completed the campers and counselors gather at a specific location for the "Captains' Challenge". Near the end of the race, the CIT captains must build a pyramid of milk crates in the pool The race ends where the campers have gathered and the captains must complete a set of tasks including at least one puzzle and one physical challenge.

"Sing Down" is a competition that has developed over years to include three songs performed by each full team (a friendship song, team cheer and a fight song), a dance by the older campers and junior counselors, poster presentations and a skit that usually lampoons the administrators, counselors and the games themselves. A time honored tradition of the OL/OS includes "bribing" the judges with the presentations of gifts (snacks, trinkets, balloons, etc) related to the theme.

THE ANNUAL AWESOMELY RIDICULOUS
GREEN AND BLUE 60 SECOND CHALLENGE RACE

This is our grand finale Color War Challenge

Set up 2 lines of exactly the same 60 second (minute-to-win-it style) challenge stations with a counselor at each station to tally up points, minimum of 6 stations, use tried and true challenges, the less complicated the better so kids can figure out what to do immediately at each station without directions. We set up the stations on the long sides of our sports field.

Every 45 to 60 seconds (depending on the flow) the Director sounds off with a short, loud air horn blast. At the sound of the horn, another kid takes off running towards the first station, or transfers to the next station down the line. Spread the stations out enough so there is a short running element to the race. Positioned at the end of the last challenge station is a runway to a long tarp, counselors stand on each side with buckets of water (and a few drops of baby oil), the kids hit the tarp running, one at a time, slide down the tarp, grab a bat, dizzy bat in circles at least 5 times or more if they have it in them then race off to the finish line and drop in the grass. Points are accumulated at each 60 second station and the winner is announced after the points are tallied at the closing Color War ceremony.

Note: Since the transfers of stations are controlled by the air horn the "speed" element enables more point accumulation, the end of the race slide & dizzy bat don't add any points to the scores, it's JUST FOR FUN!

ROPE BURN

Campers watch, but only two staff members per team (reason why we split pioneering staff up) can participate. We have two poles, which we tie two ropes at the top. Each rope is worth points, the higher one being worth more points. And yes I have seen one team burn the first one and the second one burning the highest one before the other team. Makes it more exciting.

AX HUNT

Big honor if you find it. A few days before our color war breaks two senior staff take the Ax which is in the dining room and find a spot on camp. They dig a hole about 1 foot deep and bury the Ax. Only our current 9 graders are allowed to search for the Ax. They select about 6 campers each meal to go out for 15 minutes looking for it, with clues that are given to them at the start of each meal. At each meal the points for the Ax decreases, as they are given more clues. The camper that finds the Ax then runs back to the dining room where the rest of the team is waiting. It's the biggest honor to have as a camper, as your name goes on a board in the dining room which dates back to the 60's. I have goosebumps talking about this event.

APACHE RELAY

Another event which is huge and worth 100 points. Imagine a 4x4 100 meter relay. Now imagine in-between those kids running to different areas on camp, and when they get to each area there is an activity set up, like lay up shots, making a bed, climbing the wall, eating pudding etc. This event lasts for about 3 hours, and involves every camper on camp. Will take up half your day for sure.

BUCKET FILL

One of those activities that the kids will be so excited to fill a garage can up with lake water. Sounds exciting right, but it really is. Each team makes two lines, one boys and one girls. They then assign 4 runners (into water) from the oldest division (another honor to do). They have to run and jump in the lake fill up their bowl and pass it to the first child in the line. Each child continues to pass this bowl along the line to the end and dumps the water in the bucket. An amazing event to see.

TUG-OF-WAR

Simple as it sounds, by division of course, and even have a staff one at the end.

EQUIPMENT HUNT

BEST event for any athletics director. We take the campers and send them out (time frame) and they collect as much equipment as possible, each item they get one point. The team that collects the most points then wins 50 points for their team. Best part is that all the equipment is collected, and the kids find equipment that you would have never found at the end of camp.

SING

This is how we end the color war on the 5th night. During the 5 days the teams are also putting together a show which is related to their team name and involves every camper and staff on their team, this is where the dance instructors come in handy. They perform this event in front of the judges (senior staff) and only the judges that have no children attending camp can vote. Each team has to present a performance, two songs, a plaque, a speech. A banner is also presented to the entire camp at breakfast on the 3rd day which is judged, so your art staff are def needed.

At the end of Sing, we bring the teams together and announce the winner, which the kids can't wait to hear. But the special moment is that once we announce the winner the kids jump and cheer but then hug and cry, as then it hits them that camp is over and they have to go home in 2-3 days. It is always a very emotional night, but means so much to everyone.

Q-TIP SHOOTING

One of my favorite games that could easily be done as part of a color war is done the following way:

Each team is given a roll of Duct tape and a knee-high (hence forth to be known as a follicular protective device or fpd) and a pair of goggles or safety glasses.

One team member is chosen from each team who dons the FPD and goggles. On a signal the team gathers around that team member's head and begins to build a sticky side out helmet using only the roll of duct tape. Upon a second signal, all helmet construction activity must cease.

The helmet wearing team members are then led to chairs about 15 feet from a shooting line (could each be at the center of a circle if you have a very large number on each team. The teams are then supplied with q-tips and straws. Given the proper gauge of drinking straw, the q-tips should fit nicely to then be shot spitball style.

A time limit is given and each team propels the q-tips toward their helmet wearing teammate. Helmet wearers are allowed to bob and weave in an attempt to collect q-tips that are hurtling toward them, no use of hands is permitted by the helmet wearer, nor may their posterior leave their chairs during the aerial assault. Points are awarded for the most q-tips attached to the helmet as of the end of the shooting time.

LIFE SIZE JENGA

Be aware this one involves quite a bit of advance prep but can be used year after year.

Cut a 4x4x8 block of styrofoam to smaller pieces proportioned to Jenga blocks then use styrospray 1000 to coat them and make them slick:
http://www.industrialpolymers.com/product-list/styrospray-product-list/styrospray/

The key here is to have the team, with the exception of the person currently playing, to stand in a circle with a 5 gallon pail of colored water (or if you are adventurous colored slime) with a rope attached to the bottom and a weight on the top of the Jenga stack. When the stack falls the weight falls free and the 5 gallon bucket is spilled on the team.

One additional note: in this version of Jenga you do not re-stack the pieces on top you just remove them from play.

You can leave the Jenga blocks for the kids to play a non-messy game of Jenga during free time.

CAPTURE THE FLAG (MODIFIED)

Most capture the flag games that I have seen involved 1 flag. Our version includes multiple 'flags' or balls, that kids can bring to their side. In general, same rules apply to capture the flag (2 teams, jail, etc), but in our version there are multiple balls per hula- hooped area (to keep the balls together).

Put 6-8 balls in a hula hoop at each end of the playing area. Put another hula hoop on opposite corners of the playing area. This is the jail. Mark the center line. Goal is for the kids on the teams (from 10-30 kids per team) to get all the balls to their side. If they go to the other side of the playing area and get tagged, they go to jail. In order to get out of jail, another team mate needs to run over to jail without being tagged and hold hands (they are safe) and walk back over to their side).

SPIRIT COMPETITIONS
- Best Costume for the Daily Themed days –
  - Color Day - each class is a color - great fun we get completely blue, red... kids
  - Mismatched day- just as it sounds
  - Backwards day - Always Monday when parents don't read the newsletter and kids forget. Students can just flip their clothes around and no tears
  - Holiday day - dress up for your favorite holiday garb or all your favorite holidays represented in one costume
  - Superhero day - come dressed as your favorite hero
  - Book Character Day - dress like a book character extra points given for multiple characters from the same book
  - Twin and Triplet Day - dress like your friend(s)
- Memory Verses - we are a Lutheran program and at afternoon snack students call off the memory verse for the day starting with the oldest the group who knows it the best and loudest wins the point!
- Door Decorations - each group decorates their door with a theme that represents their spirit
- Olympic Games - Crazy sports depending on them of the day -
  - paper plate ice skating
  - slip and slide distance
  - water balloon throwing
  - kite making and flying for height and creativity
  - bubble gum bubble blowing
  - frozen t-shirt try ons
  - melt a giant ice cube with a toy frozen in and retrieve the toy first
- Spirit Points - staff try to "bust" kids for acts of team spirit, citizenship towards other teams, big brother big sister, leadership, helping, best manners, being funny in an appropriate non-interfering with the class way, art, and spreading sunshine
- Talent Competition - Rounds off the event and Spirit

MUSICAL CHAIRS SCAVENGER HUNT CHALLENGE

So the jist of it is you have teams that select a number of champions. We had about 10 troops that played this. So each troop selected 2 champions. If you have 2 teams you might select more champions. We wanted more than one, so that a team was not immediately out after the first round.

- Set up 1 chair for each champion to sit in.
- Announce an item for the champions to find. ('Audience' is encouraged to cheer, and offer items or suggestions of where to find them, if they have them, but not to go get the item for them.)
- The champions must run to find the item, while gone, remove a chair. The last one to return with the item is out.
- On the next round, they must RETURN the item from where they found it, and then get the next item.
- Continue until only one Champion remains.

Ex. of items we had them search for:
- Flash light
- Fork
- Girl Scout Vest
- Salt Shaker
- Log
- Matches
- Bandana
- Gloves
- Glue
- Marker
- Egg

Basically items you might find at camp...but not necessarily things immediately to hand.

PHOTO SCAVENGER HUNT

We do some sort of photo scavenger hunt every year, where we give them clues, and they have to take a picture that proves they were in that place. A fun twist would be to just give them ridiculous clues, then have a panel of judges to award points to the pictures based on creativity, humour, how well it fits the clue, etc.

BOATS ON LAND RACE

For this activity you will need 5 canoes or kayaks and an open flat field. Tie a long piece of rope onto the front of the canoe/kayak. Line the campers up by teams with their canoe/kayak behind the starting line. Divide your campers into groups of 8-10. One camper from each team will wear a helmet and sit in the canoe or kayak and hold on! The other campers will line up in front of their canoe/kayak and hold onto the rope. When you call "go" the campers will run to the opposite side of the field while pulling the canoe/kayak and camper. First one to cross the finish lines wins!

We have done this for a few summers and the kids love it. Don't allow more than 4 or 5 boats to compete at once as the field gets full and risk of collisions occur. We have done it, where the boats must turn around and return to the start line, but there was always risk of "capsizing" and the camper in the boat falling out. It's a fun spin on a traditional relay race, but using boats on land!

MEDIC

Just like dodge ball but there is a medic on each team (the other team has to figure out who the medic is) When you get hit you sit down where you are and the medic has to tag you to let you back in the game. The game is over when the other teams medic has been hit by a ball.

WATER MEDIC

We play this in canoes with balls that float (like the ones little kids jump into). Same rules as above but there is no center line they can go anywhere in the lake.

MAN HUNT

A counselor or child (older child) gets "taken" and the other campers have to find them. They split into teams and read any clues or ransom letters left behind.

THE GIANT'S HOUSE

Ages:
Any. I've played with every age group from 2nd graders to college students and they all love this game. It's very flexible and can easily be adjusted to the age of the competitors.

Group Size:
At least two groups of five people each. You can have as many groups as you'd like. Aim for each group to have between 5 and 10 people

Objective:
Use your teammates to create the named object found in the giant's house.

How to play:
1. Divide the participants into teams.
2. Select one counselor to be the "caller." (Optional: Select one or two more counselors to act as the judges. If you are short on staff, the caller can double as the judge.)

3. Everyone stands in a circle and joins hands.
4. When the caller says "start," the circle skips clockwise while chanting twice, "We're going to the giant's house."
5. Then everyone freezes and looks to the caller. The caller says, "And in the giant's house, you find a _____." The caller will name an object that is typically found in a house, such as a car, television, bunk beds, toaster, blender, etc. Try to think of items that have lots of parts and/or moving parts.
6. As soon as the caller states the object, the circle breaks up into teams.
7. In the allotted time (usually 1-2 minutes), each team has to recreate the named object using only their teammates. For example, if the object was a television, two people could hold out their arms to form the screen, one could put their face in the screen and be the news reporter on T.V., one could have their hand on the screen and their leg sticking out to be the cord, one could lie on the ground next to the T.V. and be the remote control, etc.
8. Once time is up, each team gets a chance to explain their creation to the group. Judges then select a winner and give points. Points can either be given solely to the winner or can be doled out to first, second, and third place. Or you can give points based on categories, such as most creative, best attention to detail, most accurate, most humorous, etc.
9. To start the next round, reform the circle and repeat from Step 4. Play as many rounds as you would like, but, as with all games, remember to stop the game while the campers are still having fun.

Variations: Instead of naming a particular object, give a broad category. For example, "something that involves water." This could be a sink, fish tank, bathtub, or whatever the campers think of.

ASSEMBLE THE FLAG

When we do color war and it falls out during July 4th. We have the two teams go on a hunt for all the pieces needed to put together the flag (i.e. stars, stripes, right colors etc) and then they have to put them together. The first team to finish correctly gets the points and then we use those flags to play capture the flag team against team and there are separate points for those winners as well.

RAINBOW 6
Night time challenge

Abstract:
A game played at night with two teams competing to find stations designated by colors of the rainbow hidden with progressive difficulty.

Supplies needed:
- Glow sticks for each color of the rainbow

- Markers for each color of the rainbow
- A slip of paper for each participant in his or her team color

Time:
- 10-15 minutes to explain the game and boundaries
- 30 minutes to play

Setup:
Designate leaders for six stations, one for each color of the rainbow. Each of these stations need to be hidden with progressive difficulty. For example, the red station will be the easiest of the six to find, while the purple station will be next to impossible to find. Depending on the size of the camp, multiple leaders / glowsticks / markers may need to be used at each station to facilitate the crowds. Participants start at their home bases (usually an inside location) and receives colored slips of paper that matches their team color.

Play:
Participants have 30 minutes to search the campground for the six different colored stations. When participants find a station, they give their slips of paper to one of the station leaders to be marked by that station's color. Stations must be found in rainbow-color order (Red, Orange, Yellow, Green, Blue, Purple). Station leaders check to make sure the previous station's color is on the slip of paper before marking their own color. In cases where the previous station wasn't found, station leaders return the papers with instructions to find the previous station before returning. If a participant finds all 6 colors, he or she returns to the base and receives bonus points for the time remaining. At the end of thirty minutes, a signal is given and players return to their bases with their slips of paper to be scored.

Scoring:
Award points based upon how many colors are found. Bonus points are awarded for finding all six colors and returning to base before the end of the thirty minute period.
Colors / Points
- 1 / 1
- 2 / 3
- 3 / 6
- 4 / 10
- 5 / 15
- 6 / 21

Bonus: 10 points for every minute returned early (3 minutes = 30 points)

ROPE BURNING
Rope Burning Rules
Adapted from the Camp Lokanda Official Color War Rules 1980

1. All wood must be collected prior to the event with the cut off time for collecting being dinner.

2. After that, no one will be allowed in the wood pile or near the fire circle.
3. All wood will be placed inside a rectangle 15 ft X 9 ft, which will be placed 15 ft from the circle.
4. The fire circle will be drawn around the rope burning area with a diameter of 9-12 ft.
   a. Only 2 members of a team of 3 may enter this circle during the first 3 minutes.
   b. After that, only 1 member may be in the circle. That means only one member of the team may add wood to the fire.
5. The only fuel for the fire will be wood collected from the woods. Not allowed are any form of accelerants, hay, bark, pine cones or cut lumber of any kind. Live wood will also be disqualified.
6. The ropes will be set at 4 ft and 6-ish ft.
7. Wood over 3 ft long (judge's stick) may NOT be used until the first rope has been broken.
8. The teams will be presented with the following materials:
   a. 1 sheet of paper - New York Times or Boston Globe if necessary
   b. 5 wooden safety matches
9. 30 second penalties will be awarded for the following:
   a. Wood over 3 ft long (only during the first rope)
   b. Touching of either rope in any way by anyone or anything.
   c. Use of extra matches or paper. 30 seconds each time.
   d. More than one participant adding wood to the fire.
   e. Adding wood the pile after the event begins.
   f. Putting anything in the fire other than wood from the wood pile.
   g. More than 2 participants blocking the view of spectators.
   h. These are the only penalties and they start the moment contestants step out of the fire circle.
10. If any team seeks and/or uses information from any person other than the Fire Marshal and is penalized for improper procedure, then it is the team's mistake and the penalty stands. Only the Maccabiah Roshes or participants may ask questions or interact with the Fire Marshal.
11. If the rope has not broken and BOTH teams are out of wood, then a team of 16 campers who have been selected before the event began, and who are carrying flashlights, will be given 10 minutes to gather wood, which they alone will place in the rectangle.
    a. During this time no wood will be added to the fire as the team of 3 rest at least 10 ft. from the fire.
12. If the rope still does not break after all the wood is gone, the Fire Marshal will declare a draw.

FLAG HUNT

Each team decorates and creates their own flag in the beginning of the week. For bonus points at the end of the week we will cut each flag into puzzle pieces and hide them over the facility. That color will have to recollect their flag and put all the pieces back together, the first team to raise their in front of the camp will earn points for this activity.

IN THE POOL

We had a day of water Olympic type games at the pool. Some events were...

- Best cannonball
- Best bellysmacker
- Most creative entry into the water
- An in-water dance competition
- Dive for pennies on the bottom

BRAINS, BRAWN AND BEAUTY

We try to break our colour war activities up into three categories - Brains (thinking based activities), Braun (athletic) and Beauty (arts based)

Below are two activities from the Beauty category.

Activity 1 - Mural

1. Cover a floor or field with mural paper. It should be a decent size.
2. Get a few large tubs and mix paint with water and soap. The paint colour should be the colour of each team participating.
3. The campers must cover the entire paper in their teams paint colour.
4. At the end of the given time period whichever colour is more prominent on the mural paper wins.

You can make it more complicated by stipulating that campers cannot use their hands. It's a good idea to have a hose nearby to rinse out eyes as this one can get quite exciting.

Activity 2 - Art Attack

Supplies

- A ladder
- Old lost and found articles
- Megaphone

Instructions:

1. Two equal sized playing areas should be marked with the ladder in the middle.
2. The facilitator will go on the ladder and call out a noun that needs to be created using all of the lost and found articles.
3. Whichever team's creation looks most like the item from a top the ladder wins.

The facilitator can call out things like birds, a beach, a cat, a car, etc.

BALLOON TOWER

You can do a balloon tower building contest. Each team gets a bag of balloons color specific roll of duct team. See which team can build the biggest tower in a specific amount of time.

BACK SEAT DRIVER

Set up teams so that each team has a small bike to ride, a blindfold and a course with 3 -5 cones ahead of them equally spaced. If you don't have access to cones then make them out of milk jugs filled with sand or water. You can paint them differently for each team. The first player from each team will mount his bike and put on a blindfold, the next player of the team will be the back seat driver. The back seat driver will direct the driver down through the cones weaving in and out, and then back to the start line.

The back seat driver will now become the driver and the next person will be the back seat driver. The old driver will go to the back of the line until he becomes the last back seat driver. The first team to complete the rotation is the winner.

BALLOON HUNT

Have balloons hidden through out all of camp. Your goal is to pop the other teams balloons while collecting all of yours. Each team has a safe zone for when they find their balloons.

BUCKET BRIGADE

Each team lines up from the camp lake all the way up the hill, and at the end of each of the two huge lines is a big garbage can with a ping pong ball in it. There is a line drawn on the garbage can towards the top. We also have a large number of tin coffee cans and we give the same number to each team.

When the whistle is blown, the first team member fills up the tins with water from the lake and passes it to the next team member. The tin of water is passed up the hill continuously until it gets to the last member who is closest to the garbage can. He or she then dumps the water into the garbage and passes the empty tin back down.

The goal is to get the ping pong ball out of the garbage can first and a large number of points is awarded to the team that does so.

The Catch: The tin can MUST be held with two hands by each team member at all times. This means that they cannot be holding two tins at once, whether they are full or empty. When an empty one is being passed back down and a full one is coming, the team member must put the empty one between his or her knees and then take the full one with their hands.

Also, the water must be dumped nicely into the garbage can. Only once the water reaches the line on the top of the garbage can, can the team member attempt to splash the ball out of the can.

There are referees throughout the whole line making sure that each team member uses both hands and that they are following the rules.

ACQUIRE THE FIRE

Essentially it's a variation on capture the flag, but instead of flags, the 2 teams are trying to capture items to build a torch. So on each side of the field the following items will be spread out:

- cardboard
- different lengths of 1" PVC pipe
- duct tape
- a can (for holding the fuel and wick)
- a bottle of lighter fluid only partially full
- lighter
- t-shirt for a wick
- spray paint and/or other color decorating items
- 2 water balloon launchers
- 3 buckets of water balloons will also be placed on both sides (not near the middle line)

The goal is to acquire as many items from the other teams side and bring them back to the build zone (away from the running zone) where a selected construction team will begin designing and assembling a color themed torch. This is the capture phase. Also, teams want to steal water balloons from the other teams buckets and bring them back to their own buckets. A runner is safe on the other team's side if his hand is in a water balloon bucket.

At the end of the capture phase, the building phase will be about 10 minutes to finish off all the finishing touches to the color team spirited torch display. Both torches will be lit at the same time. An unbiased judge will award points based on categories: Largest, biggest flame, most team color, etc.

The Extinguish Phase

Teams will use their water balloon launchers and the water balloons in their buckets to shoot from the mid-field line at the other teams torch to try and extinguish the flame or knock the torch over. Of course you can add rules as you like and sculpt it to your program, but this is a great color wars game with a great visual element of the torch in these games. We played with the Lighting Phase being at dusk, so the flames could be clearly seen by all. Great multi-level game. Lots of fun.

MATCHING GAME

Set up just like a matching game would be in a book. We have pictures of each staff member on one side of the paper on the other side we have hobbies or fun facts. Teams must match the hobby/fun fact to the correct leader. The team with the most correct answer receives the most points (or two points for each answer).

If you do not have many staff, provide two or three hobbies for each one staff. This is one that campers and staff love! I typically ask my staff to give me 5 hobbies or fun facts and then I create the list, they never know which ones I will pick or how I will word it

PULL 'EM OUT

Using spray chalk, create two squares roughly 7 feet away from each other. Squares should be just big enough to stand in. One person from each team enters the square and grabs one end of a tug of war rope. The goal is to make the opponent step outside of their box by pulling on the rope or giving to much slack.

CUP STACKING RELAY

Each team member is given one cup (we use Dixie cups since so many are needed). In relay fashion, one person from each team races to a table and puts their cup down, races back and tags the next person. He next person runs and puts their cup down. The winner is the team who gets all of their cups on the table in stacking formation (8 on bottom, 6 middle, 4, 2, 1). If the tower drops, all participants of that team must grab their cups and start again. Campers get excited and try to race through this challenge, ultimately accidentally knocking over the tower and have to start over.

HUMAN BATTLESHIP (WITH WATER BALLOONS)

Hang a tarp between two poles (works well with two volleyball net poles). Teams set up on their side in 3, 4 or 5 person ships. Teams take turns throwing water balloons over the tarp. If a camper is hit, he/she sits down. When all campers in a ship have been hit by a balloon, their ship is sunk. First team to sink the other teams ships wins.

RUNNING MAN

The Korean variety show 'Running Man" is very popular among the teens in Malaysia, Thailand and a lot more countries. it really is fun and has a lot of games and ideas in it. Please Google it up or YouTube search it. I bet you won't regret. =)

We modified it a little and made our own games out of it. There's 2 versions that I've seen, but just 1 related to colours so here it goes.

We made singlets with tear-able name tags (like running man's) and divided them into green, red, blue, white, yellow groups. Each group has about 5-6 participants. Every one of them was randomly given a number, but only the game facilitators know about that. So after the game has started, for example no. 40 will be called. They'll announce over the P.A. system that everybody's target is no. 40.

So everybody will hunt for him and attempt to tear off his name tag. His group can choose to protect him, or catch him and take off his name tag. This game is also a treasure hunt at the same time. So under every name tags, there'll be something there. It's either a clue, or a bomb, or nothing. If there's a clue, the colour group can secretly keep it and find it, or make it their trade to save their lives when being hunted. If it's a bomb, the person that tears off his name tag is forfeited with the person. If nothing, then the person that name tag is ripped is out. That's all.

So after no.40 is hunted down, we'll move to no.39, then no. 38, you get the idea. So your teammates may be the next target. YOU may be the next target. So you'll have to work out strategies with other colour groups.

There's voting box too. Voting papers are placed everywhere in the playing area, which may be a whole building. If you got your voting paper, you can vote a colour group, and after 20 votes, they'll check the votes. The highest voted colour group will have to eliminate one of their own members.

How you win is to get the treasure, while you're still alive. That adds A LOT of marks to the colour group that wins.

SCHEDULE OF EVENTS
Camp Colors: Green, Blue, Red, Purple, Yellow
Each person wears a color to represent their team

Objective- to participate and accumulate as many points for each respective team

7:00 AM - Event set up
10:00 AM – Start color war

Area 1
  • Tug of War
  • Water balloon toss
  • Jump rope-a-thon
  • 3 legged race
Area 2
  • Frisbee toss
  • Stacks relay

- 40 yard dash
- Wheel barrow

Area 3
- Potato Sac Relay
- Over/ Under ball Relay
- States relay puzzle
- Wet and Wild

Tug of War
# of kids per team - 10
Even amount of kids from each age
There will be 3 ropes going at the same time. The team who pulls the flag cross their line wins.
Winner moves on, and competes until there's one team left.
Supplies- 3 ropes, definition of where the lines are, flag tied to middle of rope

Water Balloon Toss
# of kids per team- 6 (2 per team)
All ages
Teams will toss a ball back and forth and take one step back. Last team with a ball wins
Supplies- Water balloons

Jump rope-a-thon
# of kids per team- 10
All ages
Campers will jump rope. Last team to have a jumper will win
Supplies-50 jump ropes

3 Legged Race
# of kids per team- 10 (2 per team)
All ages
Each team will need to tie something around their inside ankles and stand hip to hip. They will need to run from start to finish. The first team to finish wins.
Supplies- something to tie their ankles, cone for turnaround point, start & finish line

Frisbee Toss
# of kids per team- 6
2 per age group
Each camper will take turns throwing Frisbees into targets for points. Targets will be hula hoops placed on the floor in a line. The closest one will be 10 points; the farthest one will be 30 points. Team with the most points wins.
Supplies- 15 frisbees, 30 hula hoops

Stacks Relay
# of kids per team- 10
All ages
Each team will line up and take turns stacking and unstacking cups and then running back to tag the next teamer. The team that finishes first wins.

Supplies- lots of cups, 5 tables

40 yard Dash
# of kids per team- 2
All ages
Campers will line up along the start and the first to cross the finish line wins the race.
Supplies- start and finish line

Wheel Barrow Relay
# of kids per team- 4 (2 per team)
All ages
One will have his hands on the floor and the other will grab his ankles. They will go from start to a turnaround point. Then they switch positions. (The one on his hands will be the one grabbing the other's ankles) and the first team to come back to the starting point will win.
Supplies-5 cones, start & finish line

Potato Sac Relay
# of kids per team- 6 (2 per team)
All ages
One member of each team will get in the sac, go and then come back then the 2nd team member will do the same. The first team to finish wins.
Supplies- 15 potato sacs, 15 cones

Over / Under Water balloon Relay
# of kids per team- 10
All ages
Teams will stand in a line behind each other and pass a water balloon over then under the next person. If they pop the balloon, the person who pops it has to get another balloon and start all over again. The first team to get the ball back to the first person wins.
Supplies- water balloons

States Puzzle Relay
# of kids per team- 3
All ages (older kids preferred)
The teams will stand far away from their states puzzle and take turns one by one running to the puzzle and putting one state in. The first team to finish the USA will win.
Supplies- 5 USA puzzles

Wet and Wild
# of kids per team- 10
All ages
There will be two buckets per team and a bunch of sponges per team. One bucket will be full of water and the other will be empty. The teams will line up between the buckets and the first person will be given a sponge. They will dunk the sponge into the full bucket and pass it backwards person by person to the last person who will squeeze all the water out of the sponge into the empty basket. After about 5 minutes, the team with the most water wins.
Supplies- 10 buckets, sponges

Showdown Obstacle Course
# of kids per team- 20
All ages
All events will be on the track. The campers will have to try to stay in their lanes. One kid will do one event and then run to the next event and tag their teammate.
Running with hurdles- 1
Potato Sac relay - 3
Wheel barrow relay- 2
Agility ladder -1
Jump rope skip to next event -1
Over / under ball relay – 5
Soccer pass -2
Ball into goal- 1
Anchors carry a large inflatable finish line -4
Supplies- hurdles, potato sac, agility ladder, jump rope, soccer ball, big goal, large inflatable
(Everything 5x)

Talent Show
Presentation of each school's banner and cheer
~Possible dance off?

4:00 PM- Campers go back to their respective teams
-   Event Breakdown

4-WAY CAPTURE THE HUMAN FLAG
- Using a wooded area or field divide the playing field into 4 sections.
- Put a hula hoop of the team color in the back corner. Each team will start with one or two flags of their team color in their hoop.
- As the games goes on teams will try to steal flags (humans) from the other teams.
- If a kid traveling with the human flag is tagged, the flag returns to where it was from and the kid must go to their side before trying again.
- If a human flag it tagged, they can keep running if the person who tagged them is still in.
- At the end of the game the team with the most "flags" wins!

(This is also great because the "flags" know the rules and can prevent things like puppy guarding and other forms of cheating that kids always complain about while playing.)

FIELD ARCHERY
- The archery course is set up on a football/soccer field and targets are aligned at different locations on the field. Some have balloons attached for extra points if hit.
- Archers have different distances and angles to shoot from at 4 different targets (straight on, left angle, right angle).
- Each target has a shooting line to shoot from. They must have one foot on each side of

the line when they shoot (this also promotes correct shooting stance).
- Archers are timed individually as part of the score.
- The also have one shot for distance (luckily we have a lot of room).
- Archers carry 12 arrows in a quiver – 3 shots at each target.

Shot for distance is after their last shot.

COLOR HUNT

We have about 8-10 staff hiding around the camp or at a park with a field. Each staff member has a different color marker. The kids are broken into groups of 4-8 (depending on the size of the camp) and once all of the staff are hidden, the kids are instructed to go out and find the different staff members and get the color of their marker on their hand (or a piece of paper). Once the group has all of the colors of the staff, they have to run back to the starting and that team is declared the winner.

CAMP RECORD

Last year we introduced "Camp Record" and did different things from Guinness book of records. Sometime it was a team Challenge and sometimes it was an individual.

BASKETBALL TRIVIA

Each team has a basketball, you ask the question and the first team to get the basketball in the hoop (ie. Someone runs and shoots it) gets to answer it. They get it right and they get 3 points. They get it wrong and they lose 1 point. First to X (10 or 15) wins.

Some questions:
- What animal is responsible for the most human deaths worldwide? Mosquito
- What is the name of the street you are currently on? XX Rd
- Who won the world series in 2009? New York Yankees
- What language was officially a language of England for over 600 years? French
- Of the 9 baseball players in the field, how many are allowed to call a time out? Zero,

any player can request one, but it can only be called by an umpire.
- How many states are named after a President? One (Washington)

ROLL UPS ON A LINE

Hang a clothesline or have staff hold the clothesline if there's no place to hang it. Unroll some fruit roll ups and cut them to desired length and attach one end of each roll-up to the clothesline with a clothespin. Space the roll-ups about 6 to 8 inches apart on the clothesline and make sure you have one roll up per player.

The first team member on each team will run to the clothesline and eat one of the roll ups off the line with their hands behind their backs. Once it is eaten they will show their empty mouth to a staff member before returning to their team for the next player to do the same. The first team to eat all of their Fruit Roll-Ups will be the winners.

OVEN MITT PICK-UP

The first player has on an oven mitt (or a pair, it's up to you) and they must run to the other end where they need to pick up a penny and put it in the bucket. Once they have completed the task, they run back and pass the oven mitt to the next player. Repeat until all players have completed the task.

MISSION IMPOSSIBLE

Military style game. Campers/Staff decorate themselves with as much of their color as they can. Shirts, bandanas, face paint, flats, etc.

Game Play::
- Campers grab tennis balls of their color from the far side of camp area and try to get them in the marked garbage cans in another camp area.
- They can place or throw them in.
- Each garbage can will have a different value of points and a cool military decoration with it.
- The counselors and staff try to tag the campers.
- If a camper is tagged they must raise the ball above their head and walk immediately to a designated area.
- Campers can only grab balls from the original start point.
- The further away from the start point the more the targets are worth and the harder it is to get to.
- Counselors cannot enter original starting point area and must stay in a tag only area near the garbage cans.

- There will be some staff swapping the filled buckets and crates with empty ones and returning the balls to their color tubs.
- The team with the most points at the end wins!
- Counselors cannot be biased when tagging.

Step 1 – Supplies Needed:
- Large trash cans marked for points
- 4 smaller bins marked by team colors
- Team Pennies/Flags for each team
- Wood military stands for each
- Megaphone or sound system

Step 2 - Set-up:
The idea is to make the field as awesome looking as possible. Use the soccer goals covered with a tarp, use tables covered with netting. Anything you can do to make the field a little more epic looking. It also helps to place the bins so that the campers are funneled in a specific direction so that the counselors have a better chance to tag the campers

- Place Pennies and Tennis ball tubs behind the paved pathway near the country cabins
- Place 4 milk crates on the gravel near the playground and the 4 color buckets near the score board on the other side of the field on the gravel road. These will be used as tennis ball return buckets
- Obstacles and places to hide throughout the field.
- Epic music on the camp iPod
- Noodles for taggers

Using pool noodles for tagging greatly decreased injury and danger during the game. This can be determined at your discretion.

CASTLE ASSAULT
Summary:
This game is made up of 2 different rounds. The first is castle construction. Campers use the boxes provided to make the most amazing and beautiful structure that they can with the given materials. Teams are given 8-10 minutes to build the structure. Then the round is scored. The second round is the assault. All four teams will be attacking all the other teams' structures with the tennis balls attempting to bring them down.

Set-up
- 100 boxes for each team on a tarp in a corner of the field.
- Tennis balls placed near the team tarp.
- Large arcs painted 10 feet away from the tarp.
  ○ Balls must be thrown from behind this line.

KINGS CASTLE
Equipment can look like this, we ended up buying a large set (huge hit this summer!)

Summary:
This is a fantastic night of foam swords, shields, spears and strategy. The most basic form is two teams with swords and other medieval weapons will try to kill the other team entirely without losing their entire team. There is also a king and queen game in which only the king or queen need die to end the round.

Set-up:
This will require the least amount of set up of any evening games.

- Basically clear the largest area you can for a battle field.
- Use cones to mark of the area in use

Rules
- NO HARD HITTING!
- NO head or face shots
- Body Hit (chest, back, shoulder, stomach, bottom, and hips) is a killing hit. You are out of the game
- Limb Hit (arms and legs) is a wound. 2 wounds and you are out. You will also lose that limb for the remainder of the round. (i.e. leg wound means you can only move on your knees, arm wound means you can no longer use that arm)
- The safest thing to do once a player is out is to drop their weapons, and put their hands above their head and walk to the edge of the playing area
- Tell campers there will be many rounds and to play fair calling their hits
- Day camp counselors should be helping as crowd control/ reffing.

APACHE ROPE BURN
Rope burn is a timed competition, to see which team can build a better fire to burn through their rope the fastest. This is often one of the most intense events of color war. The contestants will have their fire pits side by side and their entire team cheering them on.

Each camp has its own rules and regulations, these are some simple and general rules I have seen.
- Each fire pit is set in the middle of a fifteen foot circle.
- Only the 2 fire builders from each team are allowed in this center circle.
- The second area is a 25 foot square where the coaches will be to direct the builders.
- In this space the coaches will stack and separate the fire wood. No one is allowed in this space except the coaches. People may deposit gathered fire wood in the space without entering.
- The fire pit itself will consist of two still rods that are placed in the ground so that the rope can be three feet off the ground with a slight dip in the middle.
- The rods should be about 2.5 feet apart.

- The rope should be attached with steel wire so that I will not melt during the burning.
- To prepare the rope it should be soaked in the lake or pool then thoroughly frozen.
- Once the pit is built nothing may touch it including fire wood.
- If the fire builders, or even the fire collapse and falls into it the team will receive a penalty.
    - 1st touch 5 minutes- during which the fire builders must exit the fire pit
    - 2nd touch 10 minutes
    - 3rd touch disqualified (however they must still complete the task)
- Both teams will wait till everyone will complete the rope burn.

PART
3

SETTING UP TEAMS

WAYS TO DIVIDE THE CAMPERS INTO COLOR TEAMS
AND WAYS TO RECOGNIZE THE TEAMS THEY ARE ON

MASCOTS and TRIBES

Our camp is divided into 3 tribes, with all ages mixed into each tribe. The tribes also have mascot flags, with 2 colors on each flag. The eagles are Blue & Yellow, wolves are Red & Black, and bears are Green & Silver. The campers are told to come dressed in their tribe colors for our Color Wars day.

SORTING HAT

About 3 years ago for summer camp we had the kids break up into teams of colors. We pre-picked the teams, dividing it up so that there was an equal age range of children. We let the kids know what team they were on by copying the Harry Potter Sorting Hat idea- using a giant cow boy hat that we decorated with splatter paint. Each team was given a bracelet of their team color- the kind used at events, we got them from oriental trade.

CHOOSE A CANDY

Picking teams for colour wars or any other activity can be fun. We like to use candy as a fun way to pick teams. Have a basket with different types of candy in it. Without telling the group why they are choosing a candy have everyone pick a candy from the basket. Everyone with the same candy is a team. You can use different types of candy or one type of candy that has different colours like Starburst. If you don't want to give the kids candy you can also use pieces of coloured material or markers. It's more fun to not tell the kids what it's for that way you get more mixed groups.

BANDANAS

To pick my teams, I split them up so they're not with their cabins. They each get a bandana with their team color on it to wear all week. It helps when playing games too, so everyone knows who's on their team.

BALLOON POP

We start our Color Wars with balloons red, yellow, green, blue and purple and inside the balloons are name of each camper. Once the counselors find out what other counselors will be on their team they have to break the balloons not using their hands but only their bodies working together to find the campers that are on their list. The first group to get together wins 10 point and then it all begins!

BALLOON POP II

Have a large white canvas nailed to a piece of wood or something and then a whole bunch of balloons filled with the 2 colors pinned all over the canvas. Let the campers throw darts at the balloons to pop them and the color will show. Whatever color the camper gets on their first balloon pop is the team they are on. You could also fill the gym with balloons and inside the balloon can be shredded paper or something to signify the colors. The campers have to pop the balloons until they pop a balloon with a color in it. That color is the team they are on. Some balloons will have to have a paper say sorry try again.

FREEZE POPS

When the kids come into the cafeteria for lunch, have each table decorated in a different color, balloons, etc. then hand each kid a freeze pop (a hot commodity at our camp!) the color of their pop is the team they're on.

ANIMAL TEAMS

When kids arrive at camp they learn what team they are...We always did Blue, Green, Red & Yellow - and then depending on the theme for the year, they add that into it... For Example, if it's an animal theme... Blue Coyotes, Red Bears, Green Sharks, Yellow Ducks"... the kids are evenly distributed by age and gender so the 4 teams are even, and this is organized by Program staff before the kids arrive....at every event or activity throughout camp they can earn points for their team... (good behavior earns, bad loses - depending on the other activities there are plenty of ways you can make it a way to earn points, etc)

BUFFS FROM A BAG

I direct a day camp of 100 campers. We give all our campers and staff buffs (like the ones that they get on Survivor) that are a solid color. On Monday morning one counselor of each age group (1st-2nd grade, 3rd-4th and 5th-7th) are given a paper grocery bag with an equal amount of rolled up buffs for each color. The campers line up and reach into the bag. The color of the buff they pull out is their team color. They put the buff on and stand by the staff member who is their color team captain.

I have found that kids who have come with friends do not want to be separated from them. So we allow any camper who wants to team up with one other (sometimes we allow groups of three). Then one of them picks out the buff and both of the campers are on that team.

We also have a bead reward program where the campers earn beads to put on their camp necklace throughout the week. Those campers who decide not to pair up get the "Lone Wolf" bead. We do this because we don't want campers to just pair up because they feel uncomfortable being on their own. This way they can say, "I want that "Lone Wolf" bead. We even have close friends not pair up so they get the bead - and they are fine being on separate teams.

PART
4

ODDS and ENDS
THEMES, SCHEDULES,
TIPS and TRICKS, and OTHER CREATIVE IDEAS

WEARING THE WINNING GROUP'S COLOR

In my day camp each group is named a color and an animal (Blue Pandas). They must wear their color on competition days and then compete in various activities of that week. Such as softball games, water balloon tosses, drawing contest, tug of war. On the last week of competitions the losing groups all have to wear the winning groups color!

CHOSEN TO LEAD THE TEAM

We found that spending some extra time/effort telling Generals and Captains about their roll got them to be much more creative.

Two weeks before Color War the planning committee would gather after lights out to let the Generals know about their roll. We would park a camp van behind the dining hall and turn out all the lights in camp. Then 3 of the committee members would go and each wake up the General and 2 captains (it was typically between 1am and 3am) telling them that the Camp Director wanted to speak with them immediately at the dinning hall. As the staff arrived at the dining hall they would be blindfolded and placed into the van. Once all three were in the van we would take off and drive them all over camp with loud music playing.

After 5 or 10 minutes we would pull into a spot off a back road right behind the dining hall and take the staff out. We would have a campfire going and lots of candles. Once the staff were seated around the fire we would remove the blindfolds and ask if they knew why they had been brought here (some would ask if they were being fired!) We then would let them off the hook and tell them they had been selected to lead their team during color war, explain their responsibilities, then make them sign a contract swearing them to secrecy. We then dropped that staff off at their cabin and repeated the process with the remaining teams.

After doing this for 3 years all the feedback from the captains has been positive. They told me that they were often frighten or confused at first, but that night was always memorable and inspired them to have amazing breakouts for their team.

TIE DYED SWEAT RAGS

Buy cheap white bar towels at the grocery store. Have each team tie dye there towel using their team colour. Do this a couple of days before the colour wars competition so the kids can you use them a sweat rags throughout the day. They can also use them to wave in the air while cheering their team on.

THEME APPLIED

This basic color wars format can be applied to any theme pirate, military, mining, political parties, Olympics - as long as it had at least two teams it could fit this format. The camp I worked for did not stick with the traditional red and blue. I used orange and purple camo for the military theme, black and red for the pirates theme, silver and gold for the mining theme etc.

COLOR WAR THEMES
- ESPN vs MTV (or any two tv networks)
- Army vs Navy
- Ocean vs Safari
- East Coast vs West Coast
- City vs Country
- 50's vs 80's (or any two decades)
- Brains vs Braun
- Samurai Warriors vs Dragon Slayers

COLORED POWDER

My summer camps have never had a Color Wars/Colors Games. It sounds like a lot of fun, so I did a little research. I've found that a lot of camps that have these Color Wars/ Games run them pretty much like a field day. They break the camp into two colors (teams) and they compete against each other in games such as sports games (baseball, kickball, basketball), relay races, scavenger hunts, etc.

We thought it might be fun to end the day with a "color" balloon fight, such as a water balloon fight, but with colored powder instead. We found a recipe that I believe to be similar to the powder they use for the Color Run.

Ingredients:
- Large container or mixing bowl
- Large container of cornstarch
- Water
- Kool-Aid mix (preferably a darker color like purple or blue so it can be seen)
- Food processor
- Cookie sheet

Instructions:
1. Mix the water and cornstarch until you form a liquid past.
2. Spread the mixture out on a cookie sheet or something similar, in a thin layer.
3. Let dry completely.
4. Once dry, break into pieces and place in a food processor.
5. Mix in food processor until it becomes a powder.

OUR WAY OF RUNNING COLOR WAR

I think there are as many answers to "what is color war" as there are camps. For example, we do it late in the summer, not early, and our captains know in advance the themes and what teams they are on. They don't know exactly when it will start (or break-out), but we involve them so they can be prepared and often they participate in the break. We currently run 2 teams and 4 days; however, there was a time when it was 4 and even 6 teams. We know of other camps that have done 3 teams. I would also say there are many differences between Color War at Day Camp vs. Resident Camp. This is obviously because of the age of the campers but it is also a function of the time available for staff and campers to dedicate to the event.

Here is how we run Color War at our Day Camp:

When it will happen is always a surprise, but it is usually around the 7th week of our 8 week program. There are always some "fake breaks" leading up to the real thing! The teams are always Yellow and Blue (our Camp colors) but the themes change each year. Some themes are timely others are generic. For example, last year we did Blue Superman vs. Yellow Batman. We have also done Werewolves vs. Vampires and Monsters vs. Aliens. More timeless themes have been Fire vs. Ice, Greeks vs. Romans, and Day vs. Night.

My favorite break was actually based on a Color War break that I remember from Sleep Away Camp in the 70's (although we called it Olympics and the teams were always Army vs. Navy, yet another variation). We planned a staff soccer game with our Athletics Staff vs. All Other Staff. Early in the game, our Director went down "hurt". While he is on the ground in pain, we called the local ambulance (which was conveniently parked right outside of Camp). The ambulance arrived and backed onto the field. When the EMT's opened the back doors to take out the stretcher, yellow and blue helium balloons came out followed by the captains dressed in their costumes that supported the theme.

During the 4 days, the 2 teams compete in a variety of events for points. Some are group vs. group events, mostly (but not all) sports, that are worth a total of 25 points. Other events are Division Events or even full Camp events. The bigger the event, the more points it is worth. For example, we do a Full Camp Counselor Hunt. Specialists are given sealed envelopes with a point value and a place to hide. Then the teams move throughout Camp finding as many hidden counselors as they can. Everyone returns to our theater where we collect the envelopes. We then open the envelopes and tally up the points. Most points wins. Hopefully that corresponds to whoever found the most envelopes, but not always as the point values range from -10 to +10. Since this is a full Camp event, it is worth a few hundred points.

Other events include a swim meet, "hodge podge" events, and a giant board game or game show that we usually bring in an outside company to execute. Some camps also have an Apache Relay type event that involves the whole Camp in a relay race where each Camper performs a different "task" as part of the race. We have done that in the past but don't anymore as we have decided it doesn't work for us. That is why everyone's Color War needs to be customized for what works for their Camp. For us, it is also always evolving as we add things and replace things based on the feedback from each year's event. This way it is a tradition, but one that is always improving.

At the beginning of Color War, each team member gets a colored bandana with that summer's theme on it. The Campers and Counselors love getting dressed in their team's colors, complete with face pant, hair color, costumes, etc. The Captains also make a team banner, decorate their headquarters, and make a wood plaque that is judged and then hangs in our lunch pavilion for eternity as a memento of that year's competition.

We always end with a Song and Cheer event where each team performs an original song and an original cheer that the Captains write and teach to their own team. The songs (and sometimes the cheers) are typically based on current pop songs re-written with words for their team and the theme of the year. Four "celebrity" judges from Camp with no connection to either team scores each team's song and cheer, followed by the announcement of the winner. Overall, we work very hard to keep the competition friendly and balanced. For many of our Campers, it is their favorite week of the summer. It probably is the hardest week for our Staff to plan and execute, but it is a great way to teach many life skills and create great memories.

MARVEL vs. DC
This past summer we did Marvel vs DC Comics

We divide our camp into our colors Green and White. We then assign them a "team" theme. We then assign two generals usually senior counselors and 2 captains usually 2 junior counselors. We usually do male 2 each and female 2 each.

The camp is divided pretty evenly into either team depending on the age groups etc. This is done by me and my assistant program director.

We usually meet with just the generals the first week of camp to start planning. We feel their input is valuable. So as a team we work with the generals, the athletic director and myself and the assistant program director. Generally my assistant and I come up with the plan prior to the start of camp then meet as a team to put it into play and add whatever elements come up during this process. We generally meet once per week. The generals and captains are responsible for the implementation of the plan, their team song and cheer and any "secret" strategy plans they may have.

Throughout the week – (Usually color war goes on for 4 days.) we have various activities:
- Every morning the generals and captains have a challenge – for points. This is secret to them.
- Every afternoon we have various sport competitions with the senior counselors, junior counselors, specialist all assigned a day to compete. The entire camp comes to watch and cheer on their team counselors.
- Every day the athletic department sets up tournament competitions between the bunks for points.
- Every day the specialists do competitions within their areas – like the cooking dept does blindfold tastings – the pool does races, etc…the dock does races, etc.
- Every day we do competitions at lunch – silent lunch, etc.

Also, emails are sent home to tell the parents about the entire week's activities including the various "dress up" days we included.

At the end of each day points are turned into the Program office – we announce the points at the end of each day. Either team could be winning or losing depending on the points.

On the last day of color war – we do song and cheer competition; each team must present their song and cheer with their entire camp body. They are judged and scored – the points are kept secret.

Then the entire camp goes out to an enormous field day relay where each bunk is paired with another bunk green against white to run a relay. The first team to complete their side of the relay meets their respective general at a fire – the generals then start their fire building and lighting. The first team to build and burn a string across the fire wins the relay race. However, if you won the relay/fire you could still not win because at that time all the points from the week, are added together along with the fire/relay and then the song and cheer competition scores which were secret are revealed and then added to announce the winner of color war.

OLYMPICS THEME

When we did something like this we used an Olympic theme and used the colors of the Olympic rings for the colors. We had a one day - all day event, one day for our primary (k-2) and one for intermediate (3-5). Each team (about 50 kids) had a week to prepare a flag (we were assigned countries), a flag bearer, and a presentation for the opening ceremony. For instance, we had been working on diversity and tolerance the previous week, so our primary kids signed the Pledge and the Star Spangled banner. (Obviously we were representing the US) We also had a team cheer.

OUR COLOR WAR

For us this is one of the biggest moments for the kids, and they can't wait for it to start. I leave the breaks to the end but let me tell you about everything else.

We have two teams, the blue and gold, our camp colors. As for names each year we come up with different names, but somehow they relate to each other. Like the following:

- Golden Desert/Arctic Blues
- Golden World of Disney/Blue Amazing Superheros
- Golden Wilderness/Celestial Blues
- Golden Animation/Reality TV Blues
- Golden Earth/Sky Blues
- Manhattan Gold/London Blues

I could go on and on. As for picking the teams, well our Color War is for 5 days. During the day our campers compete in sports and on evenings we have staff games and special events. So when picking a team we (directors/Senior staff) rate our campers by athletic ability. This way the teams are more evenly split. We also split our staff depending on areas they work. For example art staff is very important during color war, as well as pioneering and dance staff. So we make sure that these individuals are evenly split up between the two teams.

Camp Banner - we have a banner hanging in the dining room, which plays an important part in color war. One meal the campers will go into the dining room and notice it gone, you see their faces light up and they start chanting "1,2,3,4 we want color war 5,6,7,8 we don't wanna wait". This is a sign that color war is very close. When the banner comes back it means that color war will break between 1 minute - 24 hours. The kids go wild when they see it.

DAY CAMP COLOR WAR THROUGHOUT THE SUMMER

Typically summer programs run Color Wars for a week or two but we chose to do ours a little different. We run our color wars the entire 7 week program and have color war day(s) one or two days a week.

On Color War days the children and staff wear face paint and dress themselves in their teams color from head to toe.

Each day that Color Wars takes place we run 3 different games or events. The 3 events range differently in points. The points are recorded on a large board and tallied up at the end of each week and the winner is declared in week seven (last week). All events and challenges consist of different games and events, for example some are relay races, some are team based games and others are individual based games.

SURVIVOR WEEK

We do a spin off the Color Wars- called "Survivor Week". It is our last week of our 8 week day camp. The campers can relate to this better than the color wars due to the TV show. We make multiple teams, instead of age groups, for the week and they compete in different tasks and sports events all during the week. Points are awarded and special activities and events occur daily and at the end of the week.

Details:

1. The first 7 weeks campers are grouped by ages, 7-15 yrs., but the last week they are grouped by Teams with multiple ages in them. The counselors the week before meet and get to pick their team. This is a nice benefit to them as they have been given groups all summer, and love to pick the kids they want. Some trading and bartering goes on, but our camp director has final say. This is done Friday after the 7th week and we do pizza for everyone. Kind of an end of the summer booster for the staff.

2. Campers find out their teams at flag rising, Monday morning, at a special induction ceremony. It is a big deal, and we start with the younger campers first and work up to the older campers. Announcing one child per team, for all teams and then going around again.

3. The teams then spend Monday morning getting to know one another, and creating their team flag, colors, song, and cheer. This will be used throughout the week for competitions. This time each morning is known as Team Time. Counselors can use it for preparing for competitions, team building, or other fun activities.

4. The morning activity period is a choice activity, compared to a sign up period like the rest of the summer. This gives the campers that have been with us all summer a change, and ends the summer on a positive note, as they are doing different activities of their choice in the mornings.

5. The afternoon- after lunch is set aside for competition activities. These are all the regular activities that have been done all summer, from arts & crafts to soccer. Anything can become a competition. A child of the same age from each team is selected to compete in an activity, example- beginning part of the afternoon there are enough age appropriate activities, for all campers to participate in. Art projects that are then judged, team-building activities, Lego building, card games, sports events.

6. The second half of the camp is a large group activity, or relay races. This time includes all campers, or depending on the activity, age groupings of older and younger, with one group participating and the other cheering them on. We also use the cheers and songs at this time.

7. Special incentives for winning teams daily would be a special lunch time activity or pizza party. At the end of the week the winning teams get to select counselors they want to hit with shaving cream pies, and or dump with buckets of water. We also end our week at the beach with special presentations, ribbons for teams. Special certificates for teamwork, leadership, and others, which are voted on by campers and counselors within their teams.

AT OUR SPECIAL NEEDS CAMP

Color wars at our camp seem to be a little different than the traditional "meatballs" color wars example provided. Our camp is special needs to begin with, so we have to keep our campers, cabins and counselors together at all times. Each cabin (4-6 campers and 2 counselors) is assigned a color prior to their arrival based on a balanced (male to female and 3 age groups) 4 color system. We're always a little off, but I'll explain point earning potential compensation in a bit.

Color wars begins at check in. There is no skydiver announcement (but that could be awesome...). Each camper checks in down the usual line of paperwork with the staff and then at the end, they get their picture taken, meet their counselor and any other campers that have already arrived. That's when they learn their team color and what it means that "color wars" is happening this week. This year, we'll likely be using a lot of the Harry Potter camp ideas in our theme, so we'll probably incorporate the sorting hat in the color wars "decision", when the camper learns what color team they are on.

After check in, swim test, meds, cabin setup, etc. the campers see the team-color decorated dining hall, sit at their team color table, usually get some sort of team swag like a bandana, wrist bands hat or cape (that they can earn points for being seen wearing all week). And meet the rest of their color team.

The first team challenge occurs in the afternoon of the first day. Since it's a full camp activity, it's mostly icebreakers that work with large groups and all ages. The old campers are generally more excited for color wars and their excitement leads on the younger ones. Everyone is excited to be part of a team. As a group, the teams decide on a team name (red dragons, green goblins, etc) and make up a team cheer. (We find that the girls especially love this part). The kids also make team banners and have a team flag which they carry and wave any time they are together as a team (every meal and every night).

One of the small group ice breakers we used for our old campers (ages 13-16) was to construct a boat out of nothing but cardboard and duct tape (we found colored duct tape for easy team-identification) which would be used in the opening ceremony and first team challenge. The boat must float and carry one member of your team one length across the pool! The finished "boat" design ranged from a cardboard box with tape on the bottom to an elaborate outrigger style kayak. One group even thought to make a paddle.

At the opening ceremony, the 4 color teams get together and volunteer one of the smallest kids to captain the vessel (some forced older smaller kids to go based on swimming strength). The captains are sworn in with some ridiculous oath to "paddle their ship to the best of their ability until it the safe arrival on the other side or the dramatic sinking and terrible loss of the ship". At the whistle, the captains mount their vessel and begin to paddle... and sink. Nobody makes it across in one piece, but the screams and cheers from the entire camp are simply awesome. Most kids ended up doing a side stroke rescue maneuver to drag the soggy cardboard wreckage to the other side of the pool.

The champion emerges, wet and victorious! A true hero, and has earned his team 10 points!! (The losers get 7,5,3 points respectively)

For points or tokens, we use a pirate treasure chest filled with oriental trading gold pirate coins. They were the closest thing I could find to $.01 each. I wanted something that could not be duplicated (cheated) by campers, otherwise, I would have used pennies since they were actually the cheapest and most readily available. I also considered "wooden nickels" since I do much of the camp construction, but some things are more readily purchased than made.

Throughout the week, we work in the color wars theme to every activity and really every minute of the day. Kids are challenged to be the best campers they can be. All staff and lead counselors (none of them are on teams) carry points with them at all times. Participation or improvement in activities earn points, bull's eyes at archery, home runs during kickball, reaching the top of the climbing tower, etc all are worth the much sought after golden team points. We also have a lot of kids with disabilities who should not be excluded from the opportunities for earning points that are more physical activities. We also offer plenty of opportunities for campers to be the best person they can. Holding the door for someone, playing a game with someone who was sitting by themselves, picking up trash all worth points, usually distributed discretely since it makes the camper feel even more special for earning them. Double value when the camper wasn't even trying to earn a point!

To keep things exciting, we've constructed a sort of "piggy bank" in the dining hall that kids can walk up and drop their points in. there are 4 slots, 1 painted in each color. The bank is just a flat board with 4 columns, 1 for each color, and a plexiglass front. This way, when the token are dropped in, they stack naturally so that everyone can see at a glance who has the most tokens (see paragraph below about earning potential normalization). We announce at dinner every night (after doing the math) which team won the day and which team is leading overall.

We learned through trial and error that uneven teams by age, gender and number will NEVER earn points at a similar rate. We've developed a normalization scale which basically ranks campers and compensates the teams with lesser earning potential for their shortcomings. If one team is 4000 points ahead on Monday night, you'll run the risk of the rest of camp losing interest for the rest of the week. Be careful what you get yourself into.

We close out color wars at the closing campfire by a "survivor" style ceremony. Each of the 4 flag bearers representing their team comes to the front, we say a little bit about each team, how well they've done and how many points they earned. After each speech (4,3), each flag bearer lay down their team flags to much cheering form the entire camp until 2 teams are left standing. Without disclosing which team is which, we give the remaining 2 speeches, an anecdote or two from the week and then announce the winner and 2nd place winner to much cheering and applause. A final speech reminding the campers that we're ALL part of Camp and ALL on the same team, keeps things civil and happy.

AT OUR ALL GIRLS CAMP

I have been lucky enough to experience Color War/Games at a number of camps and can't say enough about what they bring to the campers and staff. Some were full season camps who spent a lot of time and $ and a full week on theirs while others were much smaller in scale and repeated each session. But all contributed greatly to the spirit and fun of that summer.

Here is what I think are some the benefits:
- The surprise change of pace from normal daily activities was a morale boost for both staff and kids.
- Mixes up the staff a bit so they get to work with and get to know many different people instead of just with their age group or department.
- It can be used as a way to recognize great staff members and in large group cases, get to see their leadership of potential.
- Also created leadership opportunities for older campers.
- Can foster creativity and can be tailored to fit each organization. Some camps want the competitive aspect while others may want the whimsy and silliness. You are able to add things that will include all campers; there were musical and artistic opportunities as well as dramatic and athletic.
- At each and every camp it was always one of the most loved and remembered activities.

At one of my camps, which is an all girls camp of about 500, I was able to help establish the new tradition that that we call Color Games. It is a day and 1/2 of competition between four teams. It is generally a bunch of non-traditional games and activities that include a large all camp relay race, camp trivia quiz games, some wacky races in the pool and on the field, and a counselor and CIT hunt, all culminating in a presentation of theme related skits, songs, and banners by all teams which are judged and lead to final scores announcement. We also have included points for clean-ups in cabins and outside, silent lunches and a program called Pep points, which are slips of paper given out by judges to reward positive spirit and good sportsmanship.

We have always used the same four colors so the girls know to have something to wear in each. Being an all girls camp a bit afraid of competition, we had to really fight to be able to pull it off; our motto was "There is no victory without friendship".

Here are some of the themes that have been used:
* Lemons vs Limes that made Sprite!
* Super Heroes
* The four elements
* Wizard of oz games
* Soda games
* Candy games
* Circus games
* Different types of music
* Spice Girls Games
* Cops & Robbers
* East & West
* Heroes & Super Villains
* Kids & Grownups
* Aliens & Earthlings
* Angels & Devils
* Punk & Preppy
* Brains vs. Brawn
* Showboat vs. Circus
* Spacemen and Cavemen
* City & country
* Old & new
* East v. West
* Blue Thunder and White Lightening
* White Crusaders & Blue Buccaneers

The break out follows the "tapping" (covertly asking the staffer to lead the team) of the leaders, chosen by the admin team. All of this is done in secret to allow the surprise to excite the campers. The leaders then are given the tasks of choosing the themes, activities, and design t-shirts to be decorated and worn by the team leaders for the breakout and beyond. Typically you try and have the whole camp together so that you can pull off the surprise and have the captains come out in their colors.

COLOR WARS!!! We love color wars!
We have been doing color wars for three years now at our summer day camp. The first year it

was a just a week long, but now we incorporate it all summer long!

Each year we divide the staff into the color war teams and give them their bandannas. We only use two colors for our teams. Every Thursday at our camp is Color War day. All activities for that day are planned around color wars and team challenges. The very first Thursday of camp is our intro to color wars day. The staff dress up, face paint, wear what ever they want and can find in their specific color. This is when the campers find out what color team they are now on. It is based on their camp counselors color.

We then do activities that day to get the campers fired up about their color. Staff paint the campers faces, spray color in their hair, etc. Staff often try to out do one another because we have a weekly color war award for Most spirited staff and camp group. One of the favorite color war activities on the first day is: "Paint Your Counselor". Yes we let the children paint the staff in their color!! It is awesome.

Every Thursday after that is Color Wars day. Children wear their colors, paint face, spray hair etc. We then do team challenges through out the day to earn points. Example- bowling alley glow bowl they worked with us and set one or two of our color pins and the kids got extra points if the knocked that on down or got a strike or spare.

We also still dedicate one week to color wars and really amp our games up. The last Thursday of the summer we have a huge celebration with a kids challenge that involves paint war, mud pit and obstacle course.

THE MOST POPULAR DAY AT CAMP

We have just recently added the Color Wars theme to our special events day. The way it works is that our sister camp come together with us for an awesome Saturday of fun and competition.

On Friday night we have our camp dance and at the end we have an opening ceremony at the lake. The teams are chosen by assigning kids to either the Red or Black team. If you have siblings or family members you are on the same team. The cool thing that we do is once you are on a team you are on that team for LIFE! If you have kids one day and they come to camp they are on the same team you were on whether it be red or black.

We usually pick an event that every camper will watch the older children compete. This creates the stadium type atmosphere that everyone loves. Also we have a staff tug of war as the very first event. Regardless of who wins the tug of war both teams embrace and shake hands and hug to show good sportsmanship. We have a closing ceremony where the winning team is announced. The two years we have done Color Wars the black team has been the winner. This is the most popular day at camp.

"WILL THERE BE A 'WAR' THIS YEAR?"

We had never had a color war before, but two years ago when our theme was colors...we just decided it was too good an opportunity to pass up. We hadn't really liked the way the "wars" ended with one teams winning over the other, but even some of the kids had started coming over to me asking if there would be a "war" that year since it tied into the theme so well!!

I have to say that it really did go much better then we had hoped. The kids got TOTALLY into it. Since we are a day camp we didn't have any options for night activities and we also weren't sure how well it would go over so we just kept it to a one day "war".

Basically we had the kids come up with a song (alma mater), cheers, and banner that had to tie into their team name (water=blue, land=green). Of course the staff helped but the kids really came up with everything themselves-song,cheers,banners...everything. We ended up softening the blow of "losing" by singing a cheer altogether after the winner was announced and everyone got a cool treat from the freezer to sooth their aching throats!!!

Our second year was even better, the kids could feel it in the air. As time passed and color war hadn't been broken out yet they knew it was coming!!

The spirit was even more profound this year, with last year's practice, and we included sport activities to count for points. Again, nothing too exotic as our campers range from 7-12 year olds. The final "cheer-off" was a truly deafening experience (my ears ring from the memory....I could actually feel the sound waves pushing me!) and we try to make the final tally as close as possible so no one loses by a long shot.

One game worth mentioning that we did play with our staff was the frozen t-shirt game. Wet and squeeze out t-shirts, fold them and put them in the freezer overnight. The next day get staff up and see who can unfold and put on the t-shirt first. This was a great hit with the staff and gave the kids the opportunity to cheer for the staff.....everyone loved it....it's an oldie but goodie!

POINTS FOR TEAMWORK, SPIRIT and MORE

We have 3 groups in each age group and gave them a list of things they could earn points by for their group. Below you'll find that sheet.

Counselor:_____   Week: _____
Color: _____   Group Name: _____

Scoring:
- Counselors will daily give scores to their groups for each of the categories listed below
- At the end of the day the counselors will give the HC their scores sheet for the day and the HC will count it up and write it on the score board
- The winners will be announced on Friday during the cookout and will get a special treat.
- The flag or color of the group with the overall highest score will be displayed on the side of the bus, until such a time as they get dethroned.
- Electivities are not part of this

SCORE:
1. Teamwork (5 points max each)

POINTS	CATEGORY:
	Are we doing stuff together as a group
	Are we helping / encouraging each other during activities
	Do we have good sportsmanship
	Everyone doing or at least trying to do each activity
	Are we following camp rules
	TOTAL FOR TEAMWORK

2. Spirit: group name and flag (5 points max each)

POINTS	CATEGORY:
	Do we have a group name
	Do we tell others who we are
	Do we have a group sign, mascot, hand sign or flag
	Do we use the WASC hand sign during the day
	Group cheer, song or chant
	TOTAL FOR SPIRIT

3. Bonus Points

POINTS	CATEGORY:
	Helping someone outside of your group, including counselors (2 pts max per camper per day)
	Group follows Leave no trace principles (7 pts max per day - 1 per principle)
	Whole group can name the Leave no trace Principles (7 pts max per day - 1 pt per principle)
	Can demonstrate/explain a new skill learned today (1 pt per camper per day)
	Gave a compliment to someone today and meant it (1 pt per camper per day)
	TOTAL FOR BONUS
	GRAND TOTAL

At the end of each day the counselor will tally up their score and we would have the whole group meet together and announce scores as we add them to the previous day's tally. The scores were written on the side of our bus, where we meet and was visible to all throughout the day. At the end of the week, we announced the winner and they got a prize, which usually consisted of an ice cream / popsicle to ease the warm summer days.

We made a Wooden Color War Staff to hand to the winning group and they held the trophy until they were dethroned.

FIRST TIME COLOUR WAR

This roundtable is the first time I've even heard of Colour Wars and I'm so pumped to bring it to our day camps. We run week long camps that are from 9-4 each day. I'm really excited to share my ideas of this new to me concept and to receive others ideas to create an awesome summer of camps!

Here are my suggestions I came up with and I'm looking forward to the compilation.
Competitions:
- Back to the good ol' days– Three legged race, eggs on a spoon, tug a war
- Arts & Crafts – toilet paper your captain race, paper chains with inspirational words, paper airplane races, Our week at camp book created by the campers
- Fine Arts – best cheer using only the letters for TRICO CENTRE
  - camp name song
  - dance off! We love Friday morning dance parties at camp!
  - drama games, improve games
- Sports – basket ball, soccer, floor hockey games. Mission impossible obstacle course, Water games, slip n' slide races, leap frog
- Academics – millionaire game, word search swap where each camp creates a word search and they switch - whoever finishes first wins the points,
- Team spirit – each team to come up with one competition that will be done on the last day or two days of the week.

Colour War – Wrap Up:
Half day final competitions, ice cream/popsicle party, campers. What was the best of the week evaluations. Captain/General awards for greatest leader and a wrap up log book of the week to take home to mom and dad, facility directors send off.

IT ALL REVOLVES AROUND THE COLORS

Our camp is set up on a weekly basis and therefore start a new color war each week. This completion goes throughout the week and is collected through points. The color team with the most points in the end wins the camp trophy. In addition, each day a team wins the "ore of awesomeness" to know who is ahead in points.

Teams are preset based on age, gender and cabin groups. Points are accrued by team completions (games, cleaning cabin, team spirit, whatever you feel can be points). Points can also be taken away from teams from unsportsmanlike conduct and others.

The biggest thing that we have is that EVERYTHING revolves around the color game (Cheers, clothes, cabins, etc.).

We do 4 colors: red, blue, green and yellow. You can find almost everything in these four colors. We are always looking for stuff throughout the year as long as they have all four colors. For example, we have colored chairs around camp. Nothing special, but the kids love to sit in their team color's chair and we use them in games. The staff and in turn the campers get really involved. We have gone so far as selling different color items in our camp store, such as shirts and bandanas. We have pins that the kids trade as well with colors. Care packages are sent by parents filled with items of the camper's team colors.

GO ENGLAND!

I work at a one week at a time camp at present, but did one year at a full summer camp. This camp was very into color wars, and it was definitely the highlight of things for the campers. Each color (we had four) had a group of counselors and they were in charge of selecting the team's "country" for the week. We had a large amount of British staff, so we went with England.

The whole thing lasted a week, and scores were kept on a very fancy board that some LITs had constructed with turning dials behind to tell which of the four colors (red, blue, green and white) was in the lead at that point. The kids had activities in every area of camp activity.

My favorite to watch was the greased watermelon relay at waterfront. The campers were in the shallow end of the lake and had to push a greased watermelon back and forth without the use of hands as they swam from one end to the other.

I don't remember how we opened color war, but our closing consisted of all four teams singing their penned songs (taking a camp song the kids were familiar with and re-writing the lyrics for our team's country and color), and the announcement of the winners. This was followed by our end of the summer slide show and what I can only describe as a bonfire (they had the number for the year made out of plywood, raised in the air, and it was lit on fire). It was a great time to spend with campers and reminisce about the summer and see everything that had happened.

PRO SPORTS DAYS

Ours are called "Pro Sports Days" and we split our camp into 2 pro teams. Depending on the colors we used, we pick 2 NFL teams, NBA or NHL. Last summer we decided to let the kids decide their own team names and mascots. Even though this took a little extra time the kids loved it!

We too have had someone parachute out of a plane, decorated buses after fireworks, made a "Call Me Maybe" Parody video, had water balloon fights, flash mobbed, had a counselor fight and our last Pro Sports Day break we played Clue! The older campers always know it's coming so we work really hard to switch up when we break it.

This last year after we showed the Call Me Maybe video at the end of our counselor cabaret we surprised the oldest campers by loading them straight into vans and taking them to a fireworks show! We break Pro Sports Day every other week (3x a summer) so it's hard coming up with new ideas that will "wow" all of our campers! It's the most crucial part of planning our Pro Sports Days though because I truly believe it's what sparks the energy and spirit of the weekend!!

We tally up points and it all comes down to the "Tug of Peace" and "Whacked-Up Relay" at the end of the day Sunday to decide the winner because those are worth so many points! We also have Silent Dinners (Only the Admins can talk), Courtesy Lunch, and a Cheer, Clap and Song competition. Since our camp is divided (including the dining hall) all weekend our Head Boys Counselor always leads a really motivational speech about coming back together as one camp. Dinner Sunday night is always a nice full Turkey dinner and campers are allowed to sit wherever they want.

TRIBE DAY

Before directing my own summer day camp program I worked at an over night camp. At this camp we did something similar to Color Wars- called Tribe Day. This camp is almost 100 years old and celebrating tribes/tribe competitions is something that has been around for quite a long time at this camp. I cannot take any credit for these ideas as I only participated as a staff member, but it seemed like a great way to run the program!

Set up:
Each child is assigned a "Tribe" upon the first few days at camp. Once you are inducted into the tribe, you are in that tribe for the rest of your life. There are six tribes (one for each color of the rainbow- red, orange, yellow, green, blue, purple). Each Tribe also has their own symbol (red-fire, orange-sun, yellow-corn, green-tree, blue- bow & arrow, purple- star). There are around 30 campers in each tribe varying in all ages. Staff are also assigned to tribes.

Induction Ceremony:
Each new camper/staffer joins a tribe at the Tribe Initiation Ceremony (usually within the first couple days of camp). The campers come out to the camp fire ring one at a time and the director announces the tribe that the camper/staff member will be in. When the tribe is announced the assigned tribe cheers and sings their tribe songs/makes a big deal about a new member. No one really knows how the tribes are chosen other than the director tells the girls that he talks to "the Great Spirit" and she tells the director which campers should go in each tribe.

Tribe Leaders
After the induction ceremony tribe leaders are chosen for each tribe. These are not staff members. The campers

wishing to be tribe leader will make a short speech about why they should be tribe leader. These are usually older campers who have attended camp before. As tribe leader some of their duties will entail: organizing weekly campfire ceremony, organizing tribe duties (chores done around camp), planning evening vespers, & helping organize Tribe Day (the most important day at camp!). The tribe leaders do most of the work/planning for tribe activities and the staff are involved to supervise and make sure things run smoothly. There are sometimes evening activities throughout the summer where the campers are split into their tribes (Capture the Flag, etc.)

Tribe Day
After breakfast Tribe Day is usually announced in a creative way by the Tribe Leaders (usually by a song, skit, or random activity). After Tribe Day is announced the campers have time to get ready for the day. The campers go ALL out for this day wearing anything (and EVERYTHING) in their tribe color. (Parents are allowed to send new campers a tribe package with items to wear in their tribe colors). They wear clothing in their tribe color, hair paint, play jewlry, boas, costumes, body paint, socks, shoes, EVERYTHING is their tribe color.

Instead of normal morning activities the campers are assigned to a couple of activities where they earn points for their tribe. These are not normal activities- they are usually wacky and silly games/competitions where tribe spirit is the most important. (Think relay races on windsurfing boards, acting out tribe commercials, & making camp staff members out of clay, etc.).

Lunch is a big picnic with foot-long hot dogs and a watermelon seed spitting contest (off the swim docks).

In the afternoon there are team water relays. There are water relays of every sort in the afternoon. Staff swim relays, camper swim relays, silly beach ball relays, PFD Diaper relays, sink the canoe relays, and everyone's favorite- peanut butter relays (Peanut butter is put on a slice of bread and put on the face of camper 1 while swimming, it's passed to three more campers on their faces, and finally the tribe leader swims the last lap and eats the bread at the finish line!)

After water relays the tribes decorate the lodge for banquet dinner. They use streamers and balloons (in their tribe color of course). Support staff serve dinner to the kids (restaurant style) and have a special meal. There are traditional tribe songs that the campers sing. For dessert is an awesome ice cream sundae bar!

After tribe banquet is finished, there is tribe day closing ceremony. The ceremony is usually drug out by the staff and directors to have fun with the kids. (Staff make the director answer questions about camp, life, whatever they come up with to waste time). By this time the anticipation is growing between the campers and they REALLY want to know who's won. The announcement is made by raising each color's flag on top of a flag pole. The winning team's flag will be at the top of the pole, and will stay there until the end of camp.

By the end of the day, everyone is tired but happy!

WE DON'T CALL IT THAT

Wow – I feel a bit out of the loop. At first when I read "color wars" I wondered what that was, but then after a bit of internet search, realized it's just a "name" for what we've been doing.

Here's what we do. Each camper is assigned a team at the beginning of the week. Many times, they, nor their counselor, know what it will be until after they arrive. (This is so that we can make teams even and deal with last minute camper additions, no shows etc). Campers get a team t-shirt that is color coordinated. They also will get a team color bead that they will wear all week long. Some campers have been known to wear it until the next summer! Campers compete all week in a wide variety of events that contribute to team points.

The final event is the Obstacle Course that is worth "thousands" of points (varied depending on how the teams have done that week!) All teams participate in the obstacle course. Each camper does one event and it runs simultaneously. Our camp is a Christian camp, so campers also memorize Scripture verses that are the backbone of the team point system. Other point bearing events include:

- Tug of War
- Water Wars
- All camp games
- Cabin clean up
- In bed & quiet

The end of the week culminates with the announcing of the team winner at closing ceremonies. Winners get a pennant that is particular to that year. We have done this for over 10 years, so campers really "covet" the team champion's pennant.

HARRY POTTER STYLE

So our color war revolves around the Harry potter theme making use of the 4 houses Griffindor Hufflepuff, Ravenclaw and Slytheryn. We like that it encourages imagination in our younger campers and an interest in reading to our older campers. It runs during a two week session with the first week being a lot of the set up and the second being competition ending in two big events one for our older campers and one for our younger campers. (We have around 550 campers from preschool to entering 8th grade)

Week one:
All campers are assigned a house (we find its better to have kids assigned before we announce which house or staff will be in) we will have messages from Hogwarts read during opening and build suspense until Thursday when we announce our Generals and Assistant Generals.

We set up a sorting had and have a staff member call down the names and then one by one sort them in front of everyone. No staff know which house they will be in until that morning (this helps build anticipation for the staff). We hand pick the staff for balance and choose the team leaders that understand how to keep a fair sportsmanlike competition.

On the first Friday we have our opening ceremony in the morning the campers come dressed in their team colors and we have facepaint available as well as banners. After everyone has checked in they separate into their teams and get ready to march to the amphitheatre. We blast Harry Potter music and they make their way down. Once everyone is in there we have the running of the torch and recite the sportsmanship oath we created. The Generals say a few words and we light a fire in the middle of our pond. After this event campers then start earning points for their team at specialty area - it could be trivia, a dance off, a race, we have even had staff set up a Quidditch game.

Week Two:
Every morning during the second week we go over the scores for each house. We also have them compete by pulling up a member of each team and have them compete with the minute to win it games. Sometimes we will pull staff for the more ridiculous activities.

During Wednesday's opening we have a massive Tug of War. We run a different bracket for lower middle and upper camp as well as a staff bracket. During our Parent's night we call parents up to do minute to win it games for their camper's team and award points for attendance.

One year we had a great performer do a funny version of a wizard class based on the Harry Potter world - the kids ate it up. One of the favorite songs at our camp is black socks, and if your familiar with Harry freeing the House elf with a sock, we decided to hide black socks all over camp each day with a piece of paper with point on it each day. The camper to find them earns point for their house. The campers were looking everywhere for socks.

I almost forgot the trash clean up challenge. We set up 4 trash cans and give the campers 45 minutes to collect as much trash off the ground for their team this is a great way to make friends with your grounds keeper and give the kids point for their teams.

On the last day we run two big events the first is for our "Potion Quest" for our preschoolers through second graders. During the quest the campers travel by team along a well marked trail (I use the construction marking paints in house colors). Along the trail they search for potion ingredients (photo copied pictures I have them color after their projects are done in arts and crafts). Each house starts at a different time. After a team sets out I have two CIT's follow and put down the ingredients for the next team on the trail. Along the way teams will encounter professors at trail forks and bridges where they need to solve riddles, answer trivia, sing a song or whatever my staff can think up that year to earn brooms, a wand and some other special big point item. I let the staff choose. My only requirement is that they go over the top get dressed up and have fun.

The last stop is on Dragon Island where they need to collect dragon snot for their potion (we have and island in our pond with a bridge. I made a cardboard dragon a few years ago and give him a new paint job every year to freshen him up and then hide him on the island. The snot is just liquid dish soap I put in his nose and the team gets a Ziploc bag with a q-tip to collect a sample. The kids love it). When they are done they count up their points and submit them to be announced during the closing ceremony.

The second event that we run is for our 3rd grade and up campers. It's a massive 4 way capture the flag. We have two judges in each of the four areas and the teams don't know which area they will have until that day (we use white lime to put down the boundary lines leaving a neutral zone by our bath house for easy access of the lav and water fountain. Each section is then labeled with Construction paint by house color and letter.

It runs for around an hour and 30 minutes and we do a free jail break half way through. Each team has one large flag and 50 small flags there is a whole rule book discussing distances from flags and jails as well as which staff are worth more points (please feel free to e-mail me you would like a copy).

At the end all the campers go to the amphitheatre for freeze pops while the judges review the scores. We then announce the house scores reminding them of all the fun they had during the two weeks.

SUPERHERO WEEK
Group Name: _____

Color/Superhero Represented: _____

Your group can complete the action up to three times. A new witness must sign off each time you complete a task. If you can fill your whole board by the end of the week, we will have a special Friday snack! For things like songs, give five reasons why, and cheers, you must come up with different ones each time.

Action	Time/Place	Witness	Witness	Witness
Picked up trash				
Make up a song & sing it for people				
Make a cheer and show it to people				
Paint our color on other counselors (with their permission only)				
Everyone wore our color today				
We showed up on time to an activity				
Everyone gave a director a high five!				
Everyone danced in assembly				
Said the "superhero" grace before we ate lunch				

Walked between activities silently
like secret agent spies

As a group we came up with five
reasons why Jesus is our Superhero!

Opening Ceremonies

We always began the week with a large group assembly where we'd introduce the team captains and start earning some points.

Deal or No Deal

The most well received opening day game was our version of Deal or No Deal. We'd hang file folders (our version of briefcases!) with random point values in them in rows on a black board (you could use a wall, white board, anything) and then run the game like the TV show was played including having our emcee take "calls" from the banker upping the bets. As the captains picked the folders, we just opened them up so the values showed. The most fun was making some of the points in the folders be things like "-5 points" or "10 points to the OTHER team" that kept the suspense alive. Of course, having energetic counselor/captains who know how to get the campers involved is key. If you've never watched Deal or No Deal, it's on YouTube.

Fun Games for During the Week

Jigsaw Puzzle contests - we used everything from large floor puzzles to 1000 piece puzzles that no one would ever finish. Scoring was based on fastest and total number of pieces assembled.

Frozen T-Shirts

Tie old t-shirts into knots, drench them in water and freeze them nice and hard. Creating groups of campers working together (it's hard and the shirts are cold! children don't like to touch the cold for too long so sharing worked well) the first group to unknot their shirt and put it on (one person only!) wins.

Three Blind Dice

Cover 3 large, square boxes (U-haul sells album/book boxes cheap) in white paper and put random numbers on the 6 sides (remember to use negative numbers too) so they look like dice with numbers instead of dots. Blindfold one player at a time alternating teams. The "dice" are then rolled in a large area and the blindfolded team member has to find them and roll each dice one time. The other team members can be calling out directions, but the opposing team may also call out directions making it a loud, confusing, fun time for all. After each dice has been rolled once, the total score is added for that player. Repeat with as many players as you can in the time you have. Be sure to alternate teams.

Closing Ceremonies

Over the course of the week, each team had to create one cheer and some sort of presentation for our guest celebrity judges (we used whoever we could scrape up that really wasn't around the camp too much and didn't know the children all that well). We had everything from small marching bands and once a convertible decorated like a float. Based on the level of engagement from the counselors, this was either a lot of fun or sort of a dud. Keep that in mind when planning.

We always finished big with the counselor teams tug-o-war. After all the points are tallied and the final winning team crowned, it was always time for our ice cream social party. Since we always used the colors Red and Blue for teams, one of the toppings we served for the sundaes was Purple M&M's as red and blue make purple and once the games were over, we went back to being one unified group again.

TRIBAL SELECTION

Our version, if you will, of Color War is slightly different. We have what we call tribal selection. New campers hear a quick talk about the tribes we have at camp, what their colors are, what their name means, and what their mascot is. We explain the points competition and the spirit competition. All staff and former campers have been dismissed to get "colored up."

When the talk is over, the new campers are led by a silent, torch welding warriors (staff) from each tribe down to the selection ceremony in the gym. All new campers draw a red or blue chip out of a bucket. Whatever color they draw, that is their tribe. They are initiated by receiving a colored paint strip on each cheek and a tribal bandana. In our version you are a tribe member for life.

For the competitions, we have large group games almost every evening. Sock Wars, field games, and all sorts of games our program staff create. Most of them are strategy games where the whole team has an object that will require some defense and offense. To end the week of competition, we have shorter head-to-head games done by each age group. These games are a lot like the Minute-to-Win-It challenges.

When we started our camp we wanted a sense of belonging deeper than just belonging to the camp community. The tribes have both genders and all ages and we have found our campers quickly become family and are true members for life.

IT'S NOT COMPLICATED

As I try to type this up, Color Wars sounds complicated - but it really isn't. I have experienced Color Wars in many different ways - but ultimately all had the same purpose of pitting groups against each other, friendly competitions, counselors acting crazy, campers yelling and screaming until they are hoarse, and one group claiming victory at the week's end (or the day's end).

With a camp of 100+ kids - our campers were assigned to groups of 10-14 children, each with 2 leaders. (Each group had a Sr. Counselor and a Jr. Counselor.) On Monday mornings, as the groups were getting to know each other, the counselors distributed red and blue wristbands within their groups - "allowing" friends to be together if they wanted to be - but making sure the group was divided fairly (half red and half blue). This is when Color Wars was explained/ discussed. One of the counselors represented the red team, while the other represented the blue team. Kids wore their wristband all week and were encouraged to dress in their team colors as well. Counselors kept the rivalry going by painting their faces, their nails, wearing funny wigs, crazy socks, etc. Kids made up chants to scream at each other.

For "week long" Color Wars - points accumulate during the whole week. Campers had regular camp activities each day like sports, dramatics, arts & crafts and swimming - all which had nothing to do with Color Wars. It was the final hour and fifteen minutes at the end of each camp day that the CW activities took place. Having competitive events at the end of each day kept campers interested and excited. It also kept counselors on their toes at a time when some would tend to slack off. Counselors are very competitive so it is likely they will be trying very hard to cheer their teams on to victory.

Each day at 2:30pm the camp bell would ring for Color Wars! Everyone ran around screaming and had 10 minutes to use the restroom/wash hands, grab a snack, and get their things together for dismissal which was at 4pm. All campers met on the Athletic Field (or squished into the Activity Pavilion if it was raining): Team Blue opposite Team Red.

We always started with a crazy counselor challenge (awarding points to the winning team), then split up to do the camper challenges. Virtually ANY activity can be modified for ages and abilities of campers. Sometimes the easiest activities are the silliest. Some of the activities required large numbers of campers, others had smaller groups going off to different areas of camp to compete. Teams should be balanced fairly well with each group having a mix of older campers, and younger campers. Make sure that all kids get involved. You will have kids that want to do every challenge, and some that won't want to do any! Try to keep kids as active as possible!

It's important to declare a solid point system for Color Wars. Sometimes, when lined up for relays, you will have multiple red teams and multiple blue teams competing at the same time. You might want to give 5 points for the first place team, 3 points for the second place team, and 1 point for the third place team. It would be possible for one color team to earn ALL the points if - say they come in 1st, 2nd, and 3rd.

- Relays of all kinds work well, but make sure there is minimal down time. If the groups are too large, and kids have to wait a long time for their turn - they will lose interest.
- Food / Messy Challenges are a huge hit - especially ones involving cool whip or shaving cream.
- Races putting puzzles together on top of a piece of poster board (48pc dollar store puzzles/all the same design).
- Tug of Wars
- Scavenger Hunts (find/collect items like a band aid, a Y shaped twig, a candy wrapper, a clover, a heart shaped rock, swim goggles, 3 squares of toilet paper, a #2 pencil, Gatorade cap, clothes pin etc)
- Hula Hoop contests
- Archery Challenge
- Any sports activity

By Friday all kids are revved up and anxious to hear how the points have added up. Counselors gave out awards after lunch and then all campers gathered in the Athletic Field to see which flag goes up the flag pole. Directors try to keep the color hidden until the very last minute (in a paper bag or sleeping bag sack) and then run the winning color (flag) up the flag pole. After all the hooting and hollering the winning team lines up first for ice cream sundaes. The other team is served after the Color Wars winners and they must clean up the mess/collect the garbage.

Red and Blue wristbands are available from Oriental Trading (Patriotic Sayings Bracelets).

GAME ON – WHAT COLOR WINS DAY
Designed as a Day Camp Spirit Day, camp takes on a totally different delivery from the typical camp day.

The day is based on team work. Points are issued for various activities and task that ultimately determine the winner of the day. Each camp group is pre-assigned a color and instructed to dress to the color. Bandanas in the colors are issued to the groups and can be worn, tied and used however the group chooses. Each camp group is challenged to come up with the most exciting, spirited flag that they bring to the opening ceremony on WHAT COLOR WINS DAY.

After an All Camp Meeting to announce the start of the GAME ON Day groups are given instruction to compete in various Activity Game Stations for the morning session. Stations include:
- Capture the Flag
- Kickball
- Basketball – Three Point Shot
- Archery
- Pull-Up
- and Obstacle Course

After a lunch break, campers continue with a second set of challenges to include:
- Pie Eating Contest
- Watermelon Seed Propelling Contest
- Marble Toe Fishing
- and Trail Run

Two ending activities – Four by four relays and the ending tug of war help to make the day full.

The day ends with a Closing Ceremony where the totals for the activities are reported and the team with the highest total is named the winning Color for the Year.

NEW TO OUR SCHOOL CAMP CURRICULUM
We have not done a color wars yet but this summer we plan on adding this to our curriculum! We choose the teams based on the children's age and who they like to hang out with. We believe by integrating the children it will expose them to many different people and potentially give

them the best experience possible.

We let the children pick their team names but some of the choices could be mighty blue, butterflies, tigers, lions. We want to do the color wars all throughout summer camp and tally up the points at the end of camp. So we will use one day of week for just color wars challenges but continue it throughout the camp.

The challenges for each week included:
- Capture the Flag
- Scavenger hunt
- Cool whip race (team members cover their friend in cool whip and the fastest one wins)
- Red Rover
- Grammar race (team members have to correct a word or sentence to get points)
- Suitcase race (team members have to dress in clothes and run to the end of the yard with clothes on, come back so another team member can do the same
- Clue (life sized game of clue)
- Ships and Sailors
- Hide and Seek
- Basketball
- Football
- Bowling
- Flashlight tag

We will end the color wars with a huge battle of Nerf gun war and a friendly Friday. Our friendly Friday will consist of a paper with each of the children's name and other children have to write nice things about them. We will also have a giant pizza party and the winners will be able to win a mega prize from our prize chest.

YOUTH FAVORITES

I asked some of the youth that went to youth camp for a few ideas that were the faves and here is what I got.

Each team has to make their own flag, name (has to do with the color). One year they were the green team but the name of their team was "Team enormous green rage monster"-which meant the hulk in long form lol) They also had to make their own team chant that they performed in front of everyone and got points accordingly.

Some of the games they liked best were: best/biggest belly flop in the mud pit, tug of war (over the mud pit), and a game where you tied pantyhose around your waste with an orange in it. The object was to knock a cup off each stand. Some stands were high and some were low. I saw a video of them doing it and its pretty hilarious. There is another one where they put pantyhose on head and try to knock the 2 liters over the fastest. You could probably make it into a two person per team relay to get points.

Also, I had an idea on choosing teams, or announcing it. Anyway I'm sure you have seen on Pinterest the gender reveal cake pops to announce the sex of a baby. Same concept. Everyone gets a cake pop that looks the same but when they bite into it, it reveals what team they are on. That way it's fair and a treat also.

KICK OFF SUMMER WITH A COLOR WAR

I have to say I had no idea what color wars was until I researched myself. The more I researched the more I decided that this was definitely a theme I want to try with our camp this year and maybe a new tradition. Most camps seem to end the summer with these wars, but why not start off the summer this way. It can be a way to introduce team building and kick off summer in a fun way.

I have a wide range of ages in my summer camp ranging from 5 up to 10 years of age. I have 4 councellors, possibly 5 so we can have four teams. Start by giving each team there councellor and colors. Each team will then tie die shirts or bandanas in their team color. They will also create their team flag or banner. Then let the wars begin; one day would be filled with just sports, another day can be minute to win it challenges we can have a dance-a-thon and then end with a team talent show, best group wins. This could be continued through the whole summer, who says it has to be just a week.

TEAM SPIRIT

We've been running a similar theme at our day camp for the past 4 years that we call Team Spirit, and we do 4 teams instead of 2, but basically the same idea- a week-long competition with a variety of different competitions and keep points posted each day to keep up interest. We try to vary the types of events offered so each camper has a chance to show off their strengths and interests. We've never done a "break" but will try to work one in this year. Here's a listing of the kinds of events we've used to earn points:

Traditional Team Sports and Playground Games
- volleyball
- dodge ball
- kickball
- flag football
- soccer
- wiffle ball
- capture the flag
- relay races
- simon sez
- freeze dance
- ...and the like

Goofy State Fair Type Competitions
- pie eating contests
- pig calling
- watermelon (or giant water balloon) toss
- carnival games
- frozen t-shirt contest
- instead of a dressing up livestock contest, the kids get to dress up the counselors according to a theme and get points awarded by a panel of judges (office staff)

Game Show Competitions
- Family Feud
- Name That Tune
- Charades
- Pictionary
- Jeopardy
- Minute to Win It

Scavenger Hunts
- collecting actual objects
- digital photos

Considering giving each team as stuffed animal mascot this year- teams will earn points for kidnapping them; mascots can be "bought" back by performing silly (staff approved) stunts (team members have to do the chicken dance, make up a song about their mascot and why they want it back, etc). Not sure of the strife level though...Would also love to have a skit or dance off as well (thinking Gong Show).

We end the week with a barbecue and obstacle course race a la Nickelodeon- the messier the better- slide down the sudsy slip n slide, collect your color flag out of the slime filled kiddie pool, make your way through the giant spider's web covered in Marshmallow Fluff or cooking oil and toilet paper, crawl through the tunnel lined with rice krispies and pop the balloons filled with shaving cream, water or worse.

Then once the points are tallied we award team medals (honor certificates for 4th place teams, and plastic bronze, silver and gold medals from Oriental Trading for the 3rd, 2nd and 1st place teams). We end the day with a water balloon battle to wash all the gunk off before we go home-

COLOUR GAMES

Colour Games Breakout:

We're a fairly small non-profit camp, so there isn't a budget for fireworks or skydivers or celebrities, but we did our own creative thing. Our staff and campers were informed that Colour Games would break at any point and they would know when they heard the call of the trombone (yes, trombone) from the roof of the main lodge. Once this happened, everyone knew where to run and meet so that colour leaders and colour teams could be announced (Blue Knights and Red Dragons. The staff leading the games were called the Green Giants). The following is the basic script we followed (it was definitely more exciting in person than the script lets on, but you get the idea!):

Opening Ceremonies Script

*note: our camp uses camp names, hence words like "Dolce" and "Match" and "Konk" will come up often.

Dolce plays trombone on roof of Lodge to signal the start of Colour Wars, follows campers and staff to the Haven Lawn.

Green Giants: "Colour Wars has begun!"

Match: "Are you excited to know your colours? These are your colours!"
Dolce and Konk rip down the tablecloths covering the colours.

Match: "These are your colour team leaders!"

Team leads emerge.
Little D comes out of Bunkie 1 holding blue sign, wearing robe and goes to the left side of the Haven.
Kimona comes out of the Washhouse holding red sign, wearing robe and goes to the right side of the Haven.

Green Giants: "Staff reveal your colours!"
Staff go to their colour sides taking off the clothing that hides their colour. Staff begin to make bridges with their hands.

Team Leads grab one staff from their team and get them to stand at the bottom of the hill and direct the campers once they get called to a colour team. Team Leads stand by the Haven and hand out pinnies and bandanas to campers as they are called onto their team.

Match: "Let's reveal your colours." (Points to the campers)
Dolce starts by reading a name from the blue team, Konk reads from red team. They alternate until all campers have been called.

Green Giants: "These are your colour teams!"
Teams cheer, Team Leads start teaching cheers. Green Giants get into the Green Machine (the truck).

Green Giants: "Follow us down to your first challenge."
In the evening of Colour Games Breakout day, we also had what we call the Fire Lighting Ceremony. Here's the script for that:

Fire Lighting Ceremony

Campers and staff are gathered in the Courtyard after snack. Team Leads and the Green Giants come to the courtyard.

Green Giants: "Please follow us."
Green Giants lead everyone to the Lower Playing Field. Team Leads get the campers to make a circle around the 5 burning torches.

Match: (Steps forward and picks up a torch) "This is the torch of athleticism, endurance and teamwork. This is the flame of sports."

Dolce: (Steps forward and picks up a torch) "This is the torch of creativity, imagination and expression. This is the flame of the arts."

Konk: (Steps forward and picks up a torch) "This is the torch of intelligence, problem-solving and strategy. This is the flame of logic."

Kimona: (Steps forward and picks up a torch) "This is the torch of the Blue Knights. This flame represents the Knights of the present and the Knights to come."

Little D: (Steps forward and picks up a torch) "This is the torch of the Red Dragons. This flame represents the Dragons of the present and the Dragons to come."

Green Giants: Let's follow the flames together in silence as we go to light the Fire of the Games."
Green Giants and Team Leads lead everyone into the lodge, campers and staff stand in looking at the fireplace. Green Giants stand in front of the fireplace with a Team Lead on either side facing the campers and staff.

All: (Hold out your torch as it is referred to) "The flame of the Dragons, the flame of the Knights, the flame of Sports, Arts and Logic come together to light the Fire of the Games. "◎ (We all turn and light the fire together)

All: "The games have now begun."
Campers and staff cheer, Green Giants exit. Team Leads start campfire.

Our final challenge for Colour Games was a whole-team relay. There were a number of stations set up around camp and kids and staff signed up for the challenge along the relay course that they wanted to compete in. These relay events included our three main focuses: athletics, arts and logic. Here's a general overview of the relay and the order it went in. As team members finished competing in their event, they became audience participants and cheerleaders for their other team members until the very end where everyone had to help put together a tricky puzzle. Points were awarded based on which team finished first, as well as for overall sportsmanship.

START
- Staff Run (at end of the road)
- Archery (at archery)
- Intermediate Run (10-12 year old)
- Pantyhose Relay (at UPF)
- Junior Run (7-9 year old)
- Don`t Forget the Lyrics
- Intermediate Run
- Paint By Numbers (at LPF)
- Run
- Pudding Eating (at the Courtyard)
- Senior Run (13-16 year old)
- Giant Word Search (at Cocoon)
- Hieroglyphics (at Chapel)
- Intermediate Run
- Canoe Race (at the Docks)
- Puzzle (at the Beach)

FINISH

And just to tie it all together, here's the script from our Closing Ceremonies, which happened after the winning team was announced and special awards were given.

Closing Ceremonies

In Lodge after Chapel.

Welcome!
Explain Team Awards
- Spirit
- Sportsmanship
- Most Improved
- Most Valuable
- Best Effort

Green Giants call up Team Leads to announce Team Awards
Certificates are handed out

Announce the Winner of the Games
Medals distributed
Good Games - Lineup and shake the other teams hands¨

Explain Green Giant Awards
- Leadership,
- Putting others first, and
- Being invaluable to their team

Announce Green Giant Award Winners

Nathan & Brian

Green Giants: "Please head out to the Lower Playing Field in silence and form a circle around the torch."
Pull aside Nathan and Brian explain their part in the ceremony. Green Giants, Team Leads, Nathan and Brian follow campers and staff out with lit torches.

Little D: (Steps forward and holds up a torch) "This is the torch of the Red Dragons. This flame represents the Dragons of 2012 and the Dragons to come." (Puts out the torch)

Kimona: (Steps forward and holds up a torch) "This is the torch of the Blue Knights. This flame represents the Knights of 2012 and the Knights to come." (Puts out the torch)

Match: (Steps forward and holds up a torch) "This is the torch of athleticism, endurance and teamwork. This is the flame of sports." (Puts out the torch)

Dolce: (Steps forward and holds up a torch) "This is the torch of creativity, imagination and expression. This is the flame of the arts." (Puts out the torch)

Konk: (Steps forward and holds up a torch) "This is the torch of intelligence, problem-solving and strategy. This is the flame of logic." (Puts out the torch)

Green Giants: "This is the fire of the games that has been lit by the flames of the Knights, Dragons, sports, logic and arts. You have carried the flame this week with strength, resourcefulness, perseverance, teamwork and pride. Now you will carry the flame to the games of 2013."
Little D hands his torch to Brian and Kimona hands her torch to Nathan. They lit their torches from the games torch.

Green Giants: "The games of 2012 have come to an end." (Put out the games torch)
Giants, Team Leads, Nathan and Brian up the stairs and out of sight. Mushu starts GMP.

There you have it! This camp took place over a shortened week (5 days), but it was successful enough to merit having it's own full week in (our camp sessions are generally a week long).

BUCKLEY OLYMPIC GAMES
Our Olympics Games takes place over a three day span. On Day 1, we start with the morning assembly where the campers break up by teams (we give out their color the week prior). We go over the history of the Buckley Olympic Games and what to expect over the next few days. Each

color represents a different country (ex. White = Greece; Red = China).

Events are dispersed throughout the first two days around the regularly scheduled activities. Events include: banner preparation, camp decorating, sports competition.

On the final day, we begin with an "Opening Ceremonies" with torches being brought in by the Camp Director and Assistant Director. Then each country enters similar to the actual Olympics dressed in their team color behind their banner. Each team then competes in a cheer competition and 1-2 other events in front of the full camp. The rest of the day is spent doing various activities including:

- Track & Field
- Swimming relay races
- Field relay races
- Soccer
- Basketball
- Baseball
- Trivia Contests
- Freeze Dance contests

At the end of the day, the entire camp gathers to hear the results of the competition and finish with a camp-wide dance party.

SING

As I have experienced it in a few camps color war does in fact last 3 to 5 days. This is may be because of some of the elements of SING require at least 3 days to complete.
Sing is the combination of musical and art related elements that each team will create to solidify their team spirit. Sing includes and is not limited to:
- Team alma mater – describes the teams attributes
- Team cheer – cheer to rouse team spirit
- Fight song- (different from alma mater and encompasses the ideals of the team)
- Dance- 3-5 minutes long
- Banner- usually a 3x5 foot canvas painting depicting the team
- Totem- 8 foot totem to be carved with only hand tool, should represent the team
- Skits- short plays 3-5 minutes long
- Commercials- micro plays between other events(should be funny and about prior event of the summer)
- Program book- small leaflet with each of the above programs named and listed

These 8 artistic events can be the most time consuming parts of color war and in most camps carry the most points.

AT OUR JCC CAMP

We always have a SPIRIT CHALLENGE ongoing through our 3 day color war. Judges (our specialty staff) can give points for cheering, good sportsmanship, areas being clean, etc.

For the different age groups we have different challenges. We have kickball games, volley ball, relay races, tug of war, and more. Feedback in the past had been that we had little for those campers who were not sports minded. Therefore in 2012 we added a CAKE CHALLENGE where we provided a pantry full of decorating supplies and 2 sheet cakes to each team. They had to decorate/design cakes that portrayed their color and theme (each team has a specific theme based on the over-all theme of the summer.

One summer our theme was friendship. Each team had a "sub-theme" based on that.) This was a fun/messy event. Also for the non-sports inclined we added a "recycled raft race" where teams had to build a raft and send a camper form 1 side of the pool to the other. The whole camp came out to cheer and worked better than we had planned. We also had team based Minute To Win It and a dance competition.

For the final awarding of points, the whole camp comes together. Each team presents a Song (their lyrics put to a popular song) cheer and banner. Judges award points and then we announce the winners. At the end of the day, everyone comes together for a camp-wide sing along proving that although we were divided for color war we are still one camp.

SOME THEMES:
- Olympics based
- Land vs Sea
- Grover vs Elmo
- Superman vs Spiderman
- Australia vs Canada

AT OUR ALL BOYS CAMP

We run two week sessions throughout our season. We've been running Color Wars for decades. There is an element from some that they are just too competitive. Well, we are a boys camp and almost everything is competitive. We also place a heavy emphasis on sportsmanship in both word and deed. At each of our events, sportsmanship points are awarded bases upon choices the campers make in both defeat and victory. For a number of activities, sportsmanship points are higher in number for an event than actually winning the game.

Our Time Frame:

Sunday opening night pep rally: Introduce our theme - Ex. Chaos of The Greek Gods.

We also introduce who the main coach is for each team. This coach is responsible for hyping up his team, so campers would want to join him. It is good to have a high energy person with a bit of charisma for this lead.

Next week and a few days:

The coaches start making up skits or dress the part of their team. For Chaos of The Greek Gods, they wore togas and laurel crowns. By the second Tuesday of our session, the head coaches have selected divisional coaches. These guys are major. They are the ones who will be working with the campers directed for the duration of the event. Here, all personalities work well. Sometimes if there is a really introverted guy, he can be paired up with another.

The second Tuesday of the session:

Coaches are selected and now it is time to make teams. Our tradition is to hold a draft and alternate choosing until all campers are chosen.

The second Wednesday of the session:

Before supper, campers assemble in their divisions (our age group camps). We have three; juniors from age 6-10, Intermediates ages 11-12, and Seniors ages 13-15. Here the divisional coaches take turns calling out their teams and hand out to them their team shirts. We design and have Bolduc's out of Agawam, Massachusetts make our shirts. Pretty cheap. In designing our shirts, we strive to come up with a design that campers can wear throughout the whole year and always be thinking of the next adventure at Camp Fatima.

The teams will then go to supper and they eat by teams. We usually have the Arts and Crafts guys work on banners and decorations for the dining hall. Points are awarded on how clean their eating areas are after each meal.

After dinner, we break out into age group competitions. On the schedule for Chaos of the Greek Gods, I had games called Haephrasta, Piton, and Triton. Through internet searches, some of these are actual games played in Ancient Greece. Others are just an activity I made up, but gave it a Greek name.

Second Wed Evening Through Friday afternoon:

Competitions

We try to keep everyone active and expect all to play regardless of athletic ability. As mentioned before, there is a high emphasis on team.

These are the kinds of events we run:
1. Swim meet with both swimming and boating events
2. Track meet with both running and field events
    ◦ We do not actually use a javelin, but rather a broom handle.
    ◦ We have a discus but don't use it. Way heavy and dangerous, so we use a softball.
    ◦ One of our field events is called "Closest To The Pin", We put a pylon/cone in the

field and they need to roll a bocce ball towards it
   ◦ We have a sandy area for a long jump.
What I am trying to share here is that you can make up whatever you like for your field events; it's equal for everyone.
*In regards to swimming, we have younger guys who can't swim, so there may be a golf ball hunt in the non-swimmer crib. ***Everyone participates in something. That is our rule and a good one to boot.

3. Individual Events like Archery, Riflery/BB's, Tennis, Climbing Wall, Cargo Net, Checkers, Darts, Tetherball and etc... You can come up with as many as you like. During these events it is very important to make sure you have a number of activities for campers who are not athletic.
4. Team Events like baseball, kickball, football, soccer, styx, basketball, ultimate frisbee, etc...

On the Thursday Night of Color War:

Typically, we have the teams come up with some type of performance. Skits on why their Greek God is number one and such. Lots of Arts and Crafts supplies get used here as well as some purchasing of water based body paint.

Conclusion:
We update our scores for the campers at every meal, and end all competition before supper ending with our Marathon run. 1,2, or 3 miles depending on age group.

We've run Colors Wars with numbers of campers in the low 100's to a little over 300. Anything can be tweaked and adapted to make it a good time.

THREE THEMES (CAMPER'S CHOICE, CIVIL WAR and OLYMPICS)
At our camp, we change our theme for our first session every year. We put it out on our website and Facebook for the campers to submit themes. This Color War goes through all three of our divisions. Campers only compete with other campers in their age group and we combine their scores.

Our second session has been the Civil War. We've been doing this every year since at least 1990. It is extremely popular. The camp is put into two teams in every division North and South. We have an area for bonfires and some summers with the weather permitting, the South moved down to that area as their headquarters for the Color War. The North gets tents and secures a small field on the other side of camp.

To start this Color War, we have a battle at ?, whatever we want to call it. Basically, it's a water balloon fight that have balloons numbering in the thousands. It's wicked cool to see. We line the troops up with about twenty feet of space between them and we place the presidents and generals of the two teams in the middle and then we let them go.

Our third session for many may decades has been The Olympics, each team has their own real flag and we switch things up a bit. Each team is their own team. We have four teams in our Junior division and 8 in both Intermediates and Seniors. We have devised a scoring system that is equal. It's my favorite.

AT OUR YMCA CAMP
Color Wars is our favorite week at camp! We divide the camp by groups and colors to keep a mix of ages on each team: for many years we did just two colors but last year we used all four YMCA core value colors – red, green, blue, and yellow. Neutral staff wore purple or black. For our announcement we called out the names of the groups to assign the colors. Then the teams had a scavenger hunt to find out who the general would be for their team. In previous years the generals were brought in on the golf carts with horns and flags flying.

I did hear of an idea I wish we could do: All the campers were arranged in a large circle with a white t-shirt on the ground in front of them. The staff walked around and sprayed the team color on their shirt with tie dye spray, so they knew what team they were going on.

Throughout the week groups are challenged in each specialty area of camp as well as in some of the sports. Spirit points were earned for participation and positive behavior. You did not necessarily have to win the event to win the points; this kept the week fair for all levels of competitors. We alter one day of our schedule to have COLOR WAR. A massive group event day. We have three areas of events. The groups rotate to all three areas and within each area campers compete in a variety of activities. For example:

Track & Field Area:
- Badminton
- Tug of war
- Free throw
- Relay races (rackets with balls on them, bean bags on your head, cups of water to fill a bucket)
- The final event always involves a staff on staff competition

Team Area:
- Kickball tournament
- Hockey shoot out
- Beach Volleyball
- GAGA tournament

- The final event always involves a staff on staff competition

Aquatics:
- Tube races
- Wet words or Aquascrabble or Mystery ball(My favorite pool event- I collected old tennis balls and used a sharpie to write letters on each ball. One ball had a special mark on it and was the "mystery ball". The younger kids collected balls to spell YMCA or their names, older kids had to either find words or create their own words (points for the longest word). It was my way of infusing literacy programming into camp!)
- Lane races
- Back float (timed)
- Tower of Terror (another one we made from an idea we saw in a camp brochure somewhere... We had two five foot tall PVC pipes with holes drilled all over and end caps. A ball or small pool toy was placed in each tower and the campers had to use buckets to fill the tower to be the first to get their toy or ball out. But since there are holes in the pipe you have to work together to cover the holes and fill the tower!)
- And the final event at the pool is always a race between the lifeguards and counselors!

Finale:
We have a massive relay race for staff from each color group to end the week. After the winning team is announce all four generals come together to sign a peace treaty to end Color Wars! I have attached the letters we send home, and give to the staff. The treaty reads across the top of each document. A large copy of the treaty is read and signed and displayed at camp to signal the end of Color Wars.

FULL TWO DAY SCHEDULE OF EVENTS
Outlined Schedule

SUNDAY
7:30 Wake Up – Get Dressed in your Color and Head to the Field
8:00 Calisthenics at the Field
8:15 Flag
8:30 Polite Breakfast – Please and Thank You!
9:15 Army Man Search
10:00 Field Games
11:30 Meet with Teams – Create and Practice Cheers
11:45 Send Runners
11:50 Flag
12:00 Musical Lunch – Sing everything you have to say!
1:00 Rest Hour
2:00 Meet with Teams – Sign up for Track & Field Events, Gaga, and Basketball, and Lake
2:45-4:00 Track & Field / Basketball / Gaga / Lake
4:00-4:30 Nosh
4:30-5:30 Name and Get-To-Know-You Games / Team Meeting
5:45 Send Runners
5:50 Flag
6:00 Knowledge Bowl Dinner
7:45 Knowledge Bowl by Units

MONDAY
8:00 Wake Up
8:15 Runners/ Flag
8:30 Backwards Breakfast
9:15-9:45 Camp Clean Up
9:45 Creative Morning (Plan Camper and Staff Crazy Dive, Song, Dance, Plaque, Poem, Costume, Cake, and Sign Up for Pool / Apache Events)
10:00 Cake Decoration
11:45 Runners
12:00 Silent Lunch – Shhhhhhh!
1:00 Rest Hour
2:00 Pool Events
4:45 Apache Relay
5:45 Runners
5:50 Flag
6:00 Spirit Dinner
7:00 Final Team Meeting and Dress up Judge in Costume
8:00 Final Performances of Costume, Poem, Dance, Plaque, and Song
9:30 Winners announced and Lila Tov

MEALS
Polite breakfast
The purpose is to be as courteous as possible throughout the entire meal. Points will be rewarded for politeness and helping out when possible, and deducted for rudeness and lack of manners.

Musical Lunch
All interactions during lunch are to be done through the art of song. If you would like to communicate to ANYBODY, please sing your message to him or her. Creativity and your ability to stick to song form will be the primary ways to gain points during this meal.

Knowledge Bowl Dinner
Dress nicely / classy in the spirit of a knowledge bowl.

Backwards Breakfast – kcul doog.

Silent Lunch
ABSOLUTE SILENCE! Signs and signals may be used, but no voices except the Judges and Purple Team should be heard.

Spirit Dinner
The purpose is to show the judges what team is the most spirited. No cheering will be allowed for 15 minutes so that people can eat. Anything else goes except standing on benches and tables. Points will be rewarded for positive spirit.

EVENTS

Army Man Search
The Army Man Search is a new competition at our Camp. Over 1000 small army men will be hidden around camp. After our first breakfast each team will be released for 30-40 minutes to try and gather as many small army men as they possibly can. Each team will have a team bucket on the dining hall porch. All army men are to be placed in the team's relative bucket. There are several larger figurines or toys that are worth more points. At the conclusion of the 30 minutes, the judges will look at the buckets and determine which team gathered the most army  men. The team with the most will win. LIT's, Unit Heads and Cornerstone Fellows should meet on the DH porch to help at 8:45.

FIELD GAMES

Human Blob
EVERYONE gets in a circle and crosses arms as we do during friendship circle. Then the entire circle needs to move from one point on the ball field to another point on the ball field. If the circle breaks at any point the entire team needs to go back to the starting point and start again.

Human Spiral
EVERYONE holds hands and stands in a line and one side of the line of people starts spiraling in. Once the whole team is tightly spiraled together, the team must then un-spiral. Everyone should sit down in the line when the circle has completely un-spiraled.

Hodgey Podgey
A rhythm based game where players try to complete sentences using one word at a time. Each team will play together and the last THREE campers remaining will then participate in the final game against all teams. Therefore, the final game should have 12 campers plus clash. It is important to have everyone not participating in the final game SILENT so that we can hear the hodgey podgey game and time is not wasted on confusion.

Staff Sock Tag
Two male staff members and two female staff members from each team should bring 2 of their own high socks (tiny socks are not to be accepted) and put them in the waistbands of their pants. The point of the game is to pull out the socks from opposing teams. Once a sock is pulled out of a waistband it is out of commission and no one can use it. Once a staff member has lost BOTH of their socks they are out of the circle. You are not allowed to touch other staff members - only socks!

Staff Tug of War
A contest in which two teams (each team made up of 6 staff members) pull at opposite ends of a rope until one drags the other over a central line.

TEAM MEETINGS

Team meetings provide a time where the team can plan for the events and competitions, sign up their team for future events, create cheers and excite their team. Staff members need to be present during meetings because although it is up to the leadership to keep order within the team, it is impossible for them to supervise 35 campers at all times.

First Meeting
During your first meeting at 11:30am on day one, you should be coming up with creative cheers and making sure that everyone on your team is familiar with your cheers.

Second Meeting
During your second meeting at 2:00pm on the first day, you should be signing up team members for Track and Field events, as well as Gaga and Basketball Events.

Creative Morning Meeting
The next meeting is the biggest and likely most important meeting. It takes place from 9:45am – 12:00pm. Teams will sign up for who is competing in each Apache and Pool event. Additionally, during this meeting time you will be delegating people from your team to create and later present the following (IN ORDER OF PRESENTATION THAT NIGHT):

- Costume for a Judge: Each team will be assigned a specific judge to create a costume for and will have creative morning to build the costume for their judge. They will have from between dinner and evening program to dress up their judge to present at evening program. The costumers will explain what their costume means.
  - Green: Purple
  - Gold: Michaela
  - Blue: Yael
  - Red: Jason
- Poem: A couple of team members will write and recite a poem.
- Dance: A handful of team members will create and perform a dance. The larger the participation, the better for events like this but don't over crowd the stage too much.
- Plaque: Each team will be given a 4 foot by 2.75 foot slab of wood to paint their perceived image of Maccabiah. Be creative with this, but each team will only get one piece of wood, so if you mess up, figure out how to make it work. A couple of team members will explain the meaning of their plaque.
- Song: Your team song should be something that all members of your teams are able to learn and that should be understandable to the audience when you are performing on the second night. THIS IS THE ONLY PERFORMANCE THAT THE ENTIRE TEAM NEEDS TO BE ON STAGE FOR AND PRESENT.
- Cake: At 10:00, about 4-8 team members will go to the Dining Hall and each team will be given two large, blank sheet cakes, frosting and food coloring. Please decorate your cakes creatively and within the parameters that will be outlaid for each team. These cakes will not be eaten but left out for the day for people to marvel at.
  - THEME: Comic Book Super Heroes
- Pool Dives: Each team has 2 special "dives" at pool events: "camper crazy dive" and "staff crazy dive." These are essentially creative, often funny skits at the head of the pool that end with everyone in the pool somehow. It is imperative that campers know

that there is absolutely no pushing or throwing in any crazy dives!

Final Meeting
This will be the final team meeting from 7:00-8:00pm that night. At this meeting, each team should be making sure that whoever is presenting something is ready and that everyone at the very least knows the song.

Track & Field / Basketball / Gaga / Lake Events
These events will be taking place all at the same time and one judge will be located at each location. It is essential that staff split themselves evenly between the events and will help run them. See the sign up sheet for the exact events taking place. Whenever the entire event ends, the participants, judges and staff may relocate to another event.

Track and Field
Takes place on the ball field. The 100 meter is running from one corner of the ball field to the other corner and back, and the 200 meter consists of running in a circle around the ball field to each corner twice. Participants for the long jump will jump from their standing position (behind a line) and measured where they land. For the football and Frisbee toss, a staff member from each team will hold a flag marker that they will quickly place on the ground where the football/Frisbee first touché the ground.

Basketball Tournament
Each color team will have TWO 4 X 4 basketball teams (one for Younger Division and one for Older Division). Games will be 8 minutes long or the first to 9 points. Staff will play a game of "bump"/"knockout" at the end.

Gaga Tournament
Each color team will have TWO gaga teams with 4 campers each (one for Younger Division and one for Older Division). The divisions will both play 4 games. TVs (and Clash) will play 2 games.

Lake
Each team will send 4 campers from Younger Division to paddle boat race to the buoy and back, and 2 campers from Older Division to canoe to the other side of the lake and back.

KNOWLEDGE BOWL and DEBATE
The program will be divided into upper division (older unit) (dining hall) and lower division (younger unit) (gym). Two judges will be present at each. Teen Villagers, LITs, and Staff should disperse evenly amongst both places.
- The first half of the program will be the knowledge bowl which will quiz campers on BB Camp, Judaism, Israel Day and Pop Culture. For each question, one camper from each team will come sit at the quiz table, be read the question and then write their answer on the provided pen and paper. Each camper in the unit needs to answer a question before a camper can go again.
- The second half of the program will be a debate between the TVs. Each group of TVs (both in the lower division and upper division locations) will be excused during the

knowledge bowl to create an "opening statement" no longer than two minutes presenting reasons why their color is superior. One TV will then present their opening statement to the entire division and judges with zeal and fervor.

GET-TO-KNOW-YOU and NAME GAMES
This provides a time for teams to bond and get to know each other better. It will probably be more successful if it is split up between Younger and Older Divisions. Games such as 2 truths and 1 lie can be played. At 5:30, campers may return to their cabins to rest somewhat and dress up nicely for dinner.

POOL RELAYS
Whether participating in an event or not, everyone will be at the pool. Teams should find a corner of the pool area for their team. It is important that those not participating are showing enthusiasm and support of the team; judges are not only looking at placement in the competitions but the sportsmanship and behavior as well. Every event will start on the far side of the pool closest to the boys showers.

Relays
Campers doing Free Style and Breast Stroke should be on the starting side, Backstroke and Doggy paddle should be on the other side.

T-shirt relay
The staff t-shirt must be a regular t-shirt with sleeves, and your arms, torso and head must be through all the appropriate holes. It must be fully on before they get in the pool. It does not matter whether it is backwards or inside out.

Crazy Relay
Campers doing swimming with a ping pong ball on a spoon and Spiral should be on the starting side and campers sitting on a noodle and singing yellow submarine while dog paddling should be on the other side.

Crazy Dives
Each team has 2 special "dives" at pool events: "camper crazy dive" and "staff crazy dive." These are essentially creative, often funny skits at the head of the pool that end with everyone in the pool somehow. It is imperative that campers know that there is absolutely no pushing or throwing in any crazy dives!

CIT Cannonball Competition
Each CIT will cannonball one at a time. They will be judged on: form, biggest splash and creativity.

A staff member from each team should be on both sides of the pool so that the campers on their team know where to be positioned in the pool. Remember, safety is essential at the pool! This is a stressful time for the lifeguards with all of camp at the pool - BE ATTENTIVE.

APACHE RELAYS
In the Apache Relay each team member participating must be at their station before the race

begins. Stations do not begin when the horn blows but when the runner arrives to their particular station and tags the camper. When the horn blows, the chosen runner will run from station to station collecting puzzle pieces. Their presence signifies that their team members there can begin their assigned relay. Once completed, the runner collects the puzzle piece and continues on to the next station. Once a member at a station has finished their task, they are to clean up and join the rest of their team at the location of the pie-eating contest (south side.) The teams should create a giant semi-circle facing the pie-eating table. Once the runner reaches the last station (pie-eating), they must begin their puzzle on the ground and the pie eater can begin eating when the puzzle is complete. All of camp should be on the south side hill for this exciting closing of the Maccabbiah events. When, and only when the pie is all gone, the other team leader will crack an egg over their head. The first exposed yoke indicates the winner and cheering ensues.

STAFF ASSIGNED TO LOCATIONS
- Meet on the DH porch at 11:45 on Monday
- Set up and clean up their station

FINAL COMPETITION
At the evening program at the Amphitheater each team will present their costume, poem, dance, plaque and song, in that order, that they have created. Judges in their costumes will be presented at the beginning by a representative from each team who will explain the meaning behind the costume. This is the final event to earn points and there are many to be gained here. Captains should remind their teams that it is important to be a good audience to others as judges will especially be watching for this.

Activity	Supplies	Instructions
T-Shirt Relay	• oversized t-shirt (can be dry, wet, or frozen!)	1. Teams are single file 2. 1st person puts the shirt on and grabs hands of 2nd person 3. Team members transfer shirt from 1 to 2 and so on 4. Complete when everyone has passed the shirt
GROUP Change "Categories"	None	Ask participants to group themselves based on the following options: Clasp your hands together & fold the thumbs across the top, is your right or left thumb on top?

Balloon Pop	• Buckets filled w/soapy water • balloons • Sturdy chair	1. Teams are single file behind the chair 2. Run to the bucket, grab a soapy water balloon 3. Carry the balloon to the chair and pop it 4. Complete when each person has popped a balloon
GROUP Change "Categories"	None	Ask participants to group themselves based on the following options: Fold your arms across your chest. Is your right or left arm on top?
Ooblek Challenge	• Ooblek (cornstarch & water) -can use food coloring for color wars • 2 Liter bottle	1. Teams are single file behind the ooblek 2. Grab a handful of ooblek and run to the 2 liter bottle 3. Get as much ooblek into the bottle as possible 4. 5-10 min. Most ooblek wins
GROUP Change "Categories"	None	Ask participants to group themselves based on the following options: Which leg do you put into your pants first?
Baseball/Bobbing	• Baseball bat (or equivalent) • Kiddie pool, filled w/water & peeled onions or apples	1. Spin 3X on the bat & run to the kiddie pool 2. Bob for an apple/onion 3. 5-10 min. Apples =5pts, Onions =10pts
GROUP Change "Categories"	None	Ask participants to group themselves based on the following options: Which eye do you prefer to wink with?
Pie Eating Contest	• Watermelon pies (1-2in thick circle of sliced watermelon) • Benches	1. Teams are lined up along a bench with watermelon pie in front of ea. Person 2. Eat the watermelon pie without using your hands 3. Complete when all team members have finished
GROUP Change "Categories"	None	Ask participants to group themselves based on the following options: Are you a folder or scruncher (toilet paper)

ACKNOWLEDGMENT

A huge special thanks to all the round table contributors whose submissions were chosen to be in this book.

Brent Birchler
Ali Mullers
Amanda Bline
Andrea Weikert
Anthony Pyatt
Becky Siok
Buffy Demain
Bambam
Allison Marcus
Patti Sampson
Colleen McGourley
Marisa Wojtaszek
Dov Rabinowitz
Sandy Bodine
Nicole Garrio
Michelle Paradis
Howard Hall
Mike Lewis
Alisa Lipton
David Mitnick
Niko Reikalas
Alex Sego
Beth Allen
Amanda Norris
Andrew Hurst
Ange Atkinson
Bri
Christina Mohler
Dan Rhoda
Dan Clark
Dawn Rudolph
Diane Shippell
Tory Thelen
Victoria Ketteringham
Shanelle Lambert-Rauh
Emily Melear
Ettie Cohen
Matt Saunders
Lisa Rubins
Kim Chernikovich
Karen Kluge
John Shelson

Jill Lyons
Katie Warner
Shelby Borden
Rachael Fried
Philip Drake
Elizabeth Owens
Michelle Jackson
Melissa Lim
Durice Jones
Dana Chauvin
Gus Frederick
Christie Chrunik
Bernadette Keegan
Vanessa Bullman
Liz Pearce
Erin Umeck-Zegarra
Jessica McQuarrie
Lisa Dolan
Michael Landry
Amy McSheffrey
Aaron Branine
Angela Russell
Jed Buck
Cindy Grant
Ted Carroll
Todd Goodwin
Jonathan Bernacki
Stephanie Williams
Rich Rupert
Norma Sittner
Niel VanStaden
Laura Williams
Kaylahree Mayfield
Kelly Wilson
Kimberly Mallory
John Myska
Jennifer Giessler
James Himstedt
Janet Keller
Janice Williams
Kayla Savoie
Meagan Forrest

Tracey Miller
Sue Richardson
Rebecca Jess
Paul Isserles
Steve Patterson
Tricia Kline